BUS PROFILE

ROUTEMASTER

Routemaster in the country. Seen here at Penn post office in NBC corporate livery green, RML 2412 was one of the 100 vehicles built for London Transport Country Area service, 97 of which had been transferred to London Country Bus Services Ltd on its formation in 1970. *D. M. Stuttard*

BUS PROFILE
ROUTEMASTER

ALAN TOWNSIN

LONDON

IAN ALLAN LTD

CONTENTS

First published 1990

ISBN 0 7110 1912 6

© Ian Allan Ltd 1990

Published by Ian Allan Ltd, Shepperton, Surrey; and printed by Ian Allan Printing Ltd at their works at Coombelands in Runnymede, England

Front cover:
The most numerous Routemaster type remaining in service in London is the 72-seat RML, and the life of the class is now being extended by the fitting of Cummins and Iveco engines. Seen during the glorious summer of 1989 is RML2679, one of the final batch of Routemasters to be built, on the 88 at Acton Green. *C. D. Jones*

Back cover:
The RMC-series of Routemaster coaches were closely related to the standard RM but were given a superior specification which amounted to more than the outwardly obvious items such as platform doors, quadruple headlamps or even the more comfortable seating. RMC 1458 is seen outside AEC's works ready for delivery to Chiswick in July 1962. *G. Rixon*

Preface ———————————— 5

1 Origins and background ——————— 6

2 The prototypes ————————— 14

3 Production ————————— 30

4 The Routemasters that might have been — 58

5 Routemaster retrospect ——————— 74

6 Routemaster renaissance ——————— 87

Appendices ————————— 92

PREFACE

My association with the Routemaster goes back to my days in AEC's drawing office around 1952-53, when strange-looking drawings began to appear on some of my colleagues' boards on the design side of the office. I recall seeing a steering column, not unlike the familiar RT pattern, but with a different-looking gear selector attached, and then what looked like the front half of a chassis with independent front suspension. We were not supposed to be too nosey, even within the office, but prints of London Transport drawings made it obvious that something interesting was afoot even though new RT-type chassis were still coming down the production line at the rate of about eight per week.

I cannot claim to have been directly involved but was even so in at the birth in this limited way and vividly recall the sight of RM1 when it came to Southall soon after completion in 1954. The drawing office staff were allowed a brief ride around the works yard, so I suppose I can claim to be among the earliest Routemaster passengers. I thus have a perspective on the type from its earliest days which is longer than most. I certainly had no idea that it would still be regarded as the most widely recognised London bus 35 years later, nor that it would start a new career as a model well suited to the world of deregulation so utterly different to that of those days.

My association with Ian Allan began in the same period, when I began to contribute articles to what was then *Buses Illustrated*, which was being edited by E. J. Smith, who was also at AEC at that time and whom I succeeded as editor on his untimely death in 1959. So although my main activities nowadays are centred on my work as series editor with Transport Publishing Co Ltd, it is pleasantly nostalgic to find myself involved with Terminal House, Shepperton, once more even if in much grander premises than that name implied in my day!

When my good friend and erstwhile colleague Stewart J. Brown wrote an epilogue for his 1984 book on the Routemaster in the Bus Monographs series, he talked of the type being 'unlikely to disappear before the late 1980s'. We have now passed beyond that period and the Routemasters are still there on London's streets in still sizeable if reduced numbers as well as having migrated in some volume elsewhere. Maintenance standards will doubtless determine how long some of the latter, in particular, will last but 1992 is a fashionable date for a new order in many fields. Yet who knows . . .? Could there still be operational Routemasters in the year 2000?

Alan Townsin
Basingstoke, 1990

Acknowledgements

Thanks are due to the photographers who supplied pictures and whose work is credited throughout the book. Information has come from many sources over the years, but special thanks are due to the PSV Circle for permission to quote from its records and to Capital Transport for permission to reproduce the 1979 garage allocation list.

CHAPTER ONE

ORIGINS AND BACKGROUND

Although it is now 30 years since the first production Routemasters entered service after deliveries had got under way early in 1959, the story behind them goes back much further. The first prototype had been completed in time to appear at the Commercial Motor Show at Earls Court in 1954, and the process of the formulation of ideas and welding them into the concept of a complete vehicle design began several years earlier.

Just as it is difficult to trace a river back to its exact source, so the moment when the Routemaster, or more correctly the vague idea that a new design of double-decker should begin to be developed to succeed London Transport's postwar pride and joy — the RT-type, is lost in the mists of time. The development of both models from prototype to production stages was unusually protracted, firstly by the period of World War 2 from 1939 to 1945, and so far as the Routemaster was concerned, by the sudden drop in London's need for new buses in the mid to late 1950s.

In order to understand the sequence of events, it is necessary to put into perspective the way in which London bus design, and indeed, the operation of buses in London, had developed. Horse-drawn buses became popular very soon after their introduction to the capital in 1829 and the London General Omnibus Company was formed in 1855 with the object of amalgamating the many businesses engaged in their operation. Within a few years over three-quarters of the buses working in the capital were under LGOC control and this dominance continued into the motorbus era. Effectively, the switch from horses to motors occurred during the first decade of this century and inevitably the new possibilities bred a fresh element of competition and management influenced by engineering rather than a knowledge of horseflesh.

In 1908 a merger brought two of the most successful London motorbus operators and LGOC, itself with a fast-growing fleet of such vehicles, together. The latter's fleetname 'General' was applied to most of the resulting fleet of nearly 1,000 motorbuses, which included a variety of makes and models. Experience of the shortcomings of these led to a decision to set up a bus chassis manufacturing unit, using premises at Walthamstow inherited from the Vanguard company which had figured in the 1908 merger. The combination of a talented team of engineers, several of whom were later to secure positions of prominence in the bus business including some in the United States, plus the experience of the existing combined fleet, gave unrivalled expertise.

Not surprisingly, the result was widely recognised as an outstanding contribution to bus design. The LGOC B-type was not only successful in improving reliability but also set new standards of refinement — even at that early stage, what would nowadays be called environmental aspects were seen as important by the licensing authorities of the day, at that time the Metropolitan Police. After what could be counted as a prototype version, the X-type, had been built in limited numbers in 1909-10, the B-type went into production in 1910 and the output of 2,678 over the following three years was not only unprecedented as a single-model run among British commercial vehicle manufacture, for even the major car makers had yet to reach such levels, outside the mass-production pioneers in the United States.

The possibilities of exploiting this level of output of a

Left:
**The Routemaster was the
final flower of a long history
of operator involvement in
London bus design. The 1919
K-type of the London
General Omnibus Co
pioneered the half-cab
forward-control layout so
long favoured for British
double-deckers.**

well-proved model was not lost on Albert Stanley, later Lord Ashfield, already general manager of the Underground group of companies which included most of London's tube railway and quite extensive tram routes, which took over the LGOC on 1 January 1912. The formation of AEC as a bus-manufacturing subsidiary company followed quite quickly; the concern, whose original full title was the Associated Equipment Co Ltd, was registered in June of that year.

The full story of AEC's blossoming as a major maker of both passenger and goods commercial vehicles is too complex to recount here, but two strands to its development are directly relevant to the Routemaster story. One was the close link to

London bus operation that was there from the beginning. Even though the formation of London Transport (at that stage the London Passenger Transport Board, to quote its full title) in 1933 led to the separation of AEC and the latter's fresh status as an independent company, it continued to be the principal supplier to the London bus fleet until the early 1970s. Throughout that period there was close liaison between the engineering staff at AEC's works, which had moved to Southall in the late 1920s, and that at the Chiswick works inherited by London Transport from the LGOC.

Even so, there was also a degree of independence in the thinking on vehicle design between Chiswick and Southall and there is clear evidence that this was deliberately fostered by Lord Ashfield himself. One aspect had a practical basis, for LGOC temporarily resumed manufacture of bus chassis for its own use in the mid-1920s, the model concerned, the NS-type, having begun production at AEC's Walthamstow works. More significant was the slightly later period of simultaneous development of new bus designs by AEC and LGOC in the 1928-29 period. At AEC, G. J. Rackham, one of the team that had worked on the B-type but who had pursued a successful career elsewhere including spells as chief engineer at Yellow Coach (the predecessor of General Motors bus-building division) and Leyland Motors, was appointed, again as chief engineer, a position to which he brought an exceptional type of visionary authority and obtained an unusual degree of freedom of action. His arrival in mid-1928 followed his

two-year spell at Leyland, during which he had been responsible for the design of the original Leyland Titan, the TD1 model, and his first complete new vehicle design for AEC, the original version of the Regent, incorporated many similarities in concept, some of which were also traceable to his work at Yellow in Chicago. Rackham himself emphasised to the author in an interview in 1964 that the original Regent double-decker and corresponding Regal single-decker project and its introduction in 1925 'were nothing to do with LGOC' even though it was to have a profound influence on subsequent London bus development.

Meanwhile, the LGOC engineers at Chiswick were busy on their own concept, not dissimilar in some respects though the double-decker was a six-wheeler, a type not favoured by Rackham. In effect, Ashfield had set up an internal competition within the Underground empire, although in practice, AEC won the race before it was run, in the sense that LGOC began taking delivery of large numbers of AEC-design models of this generation before the LGOC got its own-design prototypes into service. There was an element of compromise, for AEC diverted from Rackham's own preference by including a six-wheeler, called the Renown, in its new range — ironically in view of his reluctance, Rackham thereby became responsible for the most successful British six-wheel motorbus design, certainly of that era, and arguably of all time.

Thus the LGOC, in its final years, had a range of bus types — the LT-type six-wheeler based on AEC's Renown chassis, the ST-type two-axle double-decker based on the Regent and the T-type single-decker based on the Regal — all of which were substantially of standard AEC design of the period. In the last few months of its existence, the LT and ST were both superseded by a slightly longer version of the Regent, designated STL by the LGOC, and it was this model that was developed to become London Transport's standard double-decker of the 1933-39 period. Almost all of those built after late 1934 had oil (diesel) engines and transmission incorporating a fluid coupling (invariably known at the time by the name 'fluid flywheel', the term adopted by Daimler, under whose patents the AEC units were produced) and a preselective epicyclic gearbox.

So far as London buses were concerned, both of these features had largely been developed on buses of the LT class, though the standard STL oil engine was smaller, at 7.7-litre

nominal capacity, than the 8.8-litre unit used in LT-type double-deckers, either new or later for the conversion of most of the class from the original petrol engines. The 8.8-litre unit had been developed from AEC's original essay at a production oil engine and was too long to directly replace the petrol unit, requiring the radiator to be moved forward. This did not matter greatly on the LT which was not of maximum legal length for a three-axle bus in double-deck form, but was unacceptable to the Chiswick engineers for the STL, and in any case the introduction of a more compact unit while still giving adequate power was in line with Rackham's general philosophy up to that period and indeed the usual trend of automotive design.

Yet before the production of roundly 2,000 'standard' STL buses had even reached the half-way point, London Transport engineers were coming round to what was then quite a novel view, that there was merit in using a large engine but derating it to a relatively modest output in the interest of long trouble-free life. An important figure at this and successive stages of London bus development was A. A. M. Durrant, Chief Engineer (buses and coaches) who was to remain in office, latterly as Chief Mechanical Engineer (road services), until 1965 and thus through all but the end of the development and production career of the Routemaster.

In 1937, however, even the RT was little more than the proverbial gleam in Mr Durrant's eye. What amounted to an almost complete redesign of the contemporary AEC Regent chassis was put in hand at Southall, quite a number of drawings for items which were to remain current through the Regent Mark III era bearing dates before the end of that year. Apart from the larger engine, developed from the 8.8-litre unit but of more compact design despite an increase of capacity to 9.6 litres, important new features included air-pressure brakes, then rare on a British motorbus (though familiar on London's growing fleet of trolleybuses) and an air-operated version of the preselective gearbox.

A prototype chassis was built in 1938 and briefly run with old bodywork before receiving a body of strikingly modern style and appearing as RT1 in 1939. Manufacture of the first production batch of 150 buses was still in hand when war broke out in September of that year and although they entered service in the 1940-42 period, further output had to wait until the end of the war in 1945. Chassis manufacture, resumed in

1946, incorporated some changes in design but a decision to adopt a precision-built type of body, based on aircraft-production principles learnt as a result of the war, delayed the beginning of delivery of completed buses until 1947. This decision led to the setting up of special production lines at the Park Royal and Weymann concerns' works that had taken over the task of building most of the bodywork hitherto done at Chiswick.

There was an enormous need for new buses after the war years, with their combination of heavy use of the ageing existing fleet and shortages of skilled staff diverted to more urgent tasks. The limited supply of new buses in wartime were mostly of the so-called utility types, with many features which in normal times would have been regarded as unacceptable for London service. These factors ensured that the RT class

Below:
The RT was a hard act to follow. The original design dated back to 1937-39 but its real impact came with London Transport's postwar fleet programme. RT152, seen at Victoria during its first week of service in May 1947, was numerically the first of 4,674 postwar examples, mostly with bodywork of standardised design, in this case by Park Royal. *S. A. Newman*

would be built in very large numbers. It was important that the production was not disrupted, so the chassis design was virtually frozen from 1946 to the end of manufacture in 1954. In that period, the maximum permitted width for a bus went up from the 7ft 6in that had applied in prewar days to 8ft, at first on a basis of route approval but, from 1950, generally in Britain. The 26ft maximum length for a two-axle double-decker that had been permitted since 1932 was increased to 27ft in 1950, but all RT-class buses were built to the 26ft by 7ft 6in dimensions to the end of production. The bodywork showed a few minor differences over the seven-year period of postwar production but remained faithful in general concept to the 1939 original in terms of appearance, yet still did not seem dated.

Some 4,674 postwar RT buses were delivered to London Transport, to which were added 2,131 Leyland Titan models built to what can be described as a cross between the contemporary PD2 specification of that maker and the RT, with the latter's transmission (the fluid flywheels and gearboxes supplied by AEC) and air-pressure brakes plus precise external dimensional resemblance with the objective of allowing body interchangeability. Of these, 500 were 8ft wide and designated RTW accordingly — there had been plans for an 8ft AEC version, too, but this was not taken beyond the stage of a mock-up of the body, which would have been derived from the standard 7ft 6in version, whereas the Leyland version had Leyland-built bodywork conforming to RT-family appearance but of the maker's own constructional design. The remaining 1,631 Leyland chassis, designated RTL, were 7ft 6in wide and received bodywork of RT style. To augment Weymann and Park Royal output, orders were also placed with Saunders, Cravens and Metro-Cammell, but apart from the 120 from Cravens which were basically of that maker's contemporary style, these too conformed to RT appearance.

With this huge intake of 6,805 RT-pattern buses, London Transport was able to replace almost all its prewar and wartime double-deck fleet as well as the remainder of its trams. It had been decided that the motorbus was a better proposition than the trolleybus and although the trolleybus fleet continued to be excellently maintained, its future was no longer assured.

Yet in the immediate postwar period, the task of catching up with normal fleet renewals had seemed daunting. Moreover, for all the shiny newness of the RT fleet as it began to become a familiar sight on the streets, it was basically a 1937-39 design and in the normal sequence of events would doubtless have given way to a successor long before 1947. Previous London bus types had rarely remained in production for more than six years, apart from instances where war had intervened.

What was more, London Transport still had enough of its original self-confidence to retain the desire that it should hold its position of pre-eminence in matters of bus design. New ideas were gaining favour in the world of automobile design in general, among them integral construction and automatic transmission. Then there was the question of the optimum size of bus that would be needed under the changing conditions of the future.

London Transport had settled on the 56-seat double-decker as its standard motorbus type at the beginning of its existence in 1933 and continued to favour this size to the end of the RT programmes. It was about the practical limit for an oil-engined two-axle bus under the weight limitations of the mid-1930s. The first STL-type buses, petrol engined and built down to a tight weight limit, had seated 60, and some provincial municipal operators, notably Coventry and after the war, Hull, had managed to achieve this figure with oil-engined chassis, albeit with tight seat spacing within the 26ft length limit.

The relaxation of dimensions in 1950, with 27ft as the new two-axle double-deck figure, made a 60-seat capacity on a conventional front-engined chassis quite practical, the weight limitations no longer being a problem. Yet in London, with trolleybus replacement as something to be considered at least as a long-term prospect, there was the problem of what size of bus would be appropriate to replace the 30ft-long three-axle 70-seat trolleybus which was the London standard. Broadly similar trolleybuses had been chosen by several British towns and cities, partly influenced by the capacity of the trams they had replaced. The six-wheeled chassis was complex and subject to heavy tyre wear and no British urban operator elected to revive the motorbus version of the species after the war.

There was also a feeling that, in any case, a shorter two-axle bus was more nimble in negotiating London's increasingly heavy traffic and that, for central London routes at any rate, the 27ft length was big enough. The trade union attitude has also to be borne in mind — generally any major increase in size was likely to be a source of dispute.

All these factors were important elements in the background to the development of the Routemaster. In terms of the new technical features London Transport had already built up some useful experience. Several batches of trolleybuses built in the 1939-40 period were of what was then called chassisless construction, with the axles and other units attached to the body underframe, the latter being suitably designed for the purpose. Automatic gearbox experiments had begun in 1937, and indeed an STL-type bus (STL760, dating from 1935) which had been used both for proving the combination of air brakes and air-operated gear-change adopted for the RT, beginning in June of that year, went on to an automatic gearbox prototype unit in November. The latter, developed in the unlikely environment of Stornoway on the remote Isle of Lewis by a small firm of motor engineers called Miller, was not yet sufficiently well developed and after a while was converted to what was often later called semi-automatic form, with no clutch or gear-operating pedal and direct selection of the gears from the hand lever. It is an intriguing thought that, had this innovation been more immediately successful, it might have been the RT rather than the Routemaster that introduced automatic transmission to the London bus scene. As it was, the direct-selection experiments continued into the postwar RT programme, during which the Miller work, with its author, was taken over by Self-Changing Gears Ltd, the concern associated with the Wilson-type preselective epicyclic gearbox from which the Miller design was derived.

In considering the basic design features for its new double-decker, London Transport had little but orthodox front-engined halfcab double-deckers with which to make comparisons. The British single-deck bus scene was in process of being transformed, and by 1950 the front-engined halfcab layout was well on the way out, being supplanted so far as major operators' fleets were concerned by the mid-underfloor-engined bus, generally with entrance ahead of the front axle. Abroad, vehicles of similar front-end layout were already in widespread use, in conjunction with either mid-underfloor or rear engines but almost invariably they were single-deckers.

There had been earlier British ventures with what were then unorthodox engine positions and indeed London

Transport had been a pioneer user of both underfloor and rear engines, with the TF and CR classes of single-deckers in 1939. Both of these used Leyland-built chassis to designs which were so completely non-standard to the Tiger and Cub ranges to which they nominally belonged, respectively, as to be largely London designs even if based on combinations of units of generally Leyland origin. Both were also unusual in retaining what amounted to halfcab layout even though the engine was not at the front, and this concept was to have an influence on the front-end design of the Routemaster, as will be seen particularly with regard to the first prototypes. Much importance was attached to good forward visibility, particularly of the close-range type needed when manoeuvring in heavy traffic and even the standard achieved with the low bonnet line of the RT was to be improved upon if possible.

However, an earlier venture in repositioning the engine on the part of AEC had met with only partial acceptance on the part of London Transport. This was the Q-type, which had the engine mounted behind the offside front wheel, and had been intended primarily as a double-decker — a point G. J. Rackham, its designer, confirmed personally to the author. The resulting body layout, with entrance ahead of the front axle and stairs to the upper deck ascending over the offside front wheel, was almost identical to that of most present-day British rear-engined double-deckers, but was startlingly advanced for 1932, when the first prototypes were built. Much to Rackham's disappointment, the double-decker version barely got beyond the prototype stage — London Transport was the largest operator but only to the extent of having four examples plus a final six-wheel version — and even though the single-deck version was rather more successful, with 233 in London service, the episode undoubtedly left its mark on him.

Rackham's final major design was an underfloor-engined single-decker, called the Regal Mark IV and designated RF by London Transport. Mechanically, there were close affinities with the RT, with basically the same 9.6-litre engine (though in horizontal form), preselective gearbox and air brakes, but the layout was in line with other postwar underfloor-engined models with entrance ahead of the front axle in most cases. Some 700 were ordered for London service, all being delivered in 1951-53.

More directly significant in relation to the Routemaster story was the double-deck equivalent, the Regent Mark IV. This also had an underfloor engine, but was otherwise very much in line with orthodox double-deckers of the period in layout, with no appreciable overhang at the front beyond the mudguards and a conventional rear entrance platform and staircase. The full-width cab was similar to that of a trolleybus, and the only gain in passenger space from the engine position was that the cab was slightly shorter than on a front-engined model. Judged from today's standards, the missed opportunity to produce something which would have been quite closely akin to say a Volvo Citybus seems hard to understand. But the rebuff to the Q double-decker was probably still quite fresh in the memory to many of those involved, notably Rackham himself.

As it was, the Regent IV did have a clearly detectable influence on the Routemaster. Only one prototype chassis was built and it is believed to have been scrapped within the same year, 1950. Yet it had two bodies in that short life, a decidedly ungainly one by Crossley and a second, by Park Royal, which was not only evidently intended as a Show exhibit but was more obviously a pointer to what was to follow. Significantly, it seated 64, the same as most Routemasters, even though split slightly differently, with 34 upstairs and 30 downstairs, and the body profile, with front end noticeably more upright than the RT or other Park Royal designs of the time, was also akin to Routemaster practice. Operator reaction to the vehicle when sent on a demonstration tour with the Crossley body had evidently been poor and yet it seems never to have been given an airing with the second, much more attractive, body. It was completed in this form in June 1950, painted in Leeds City Transport livery, complete with fleet number 800 in the 'round figure' series of previous Leeds exhibits at Commercial Motor Shows, but not only did not appear but had vanished within a few months.

One possible reason for a change of plan was G. J. Rackham's retirement in that same month. He was succeeded by G. D. Robinson, a man who had been No 2 to Rackham since his days at Leyland, and inevitably was apt to be overshadowed by his illustrious predecessor. There were now a whole series of personalities and, to some degree, conflicting policies which influenced bus design at Southall. At Chiswick, on the other hand, both A. A. M. Durrant and his design team remained firmly in control, even though London Transport had changed somewhat at least in outward form — since 1948 it had become the London Transport Executive, and part of the vast State-owned British Transport Commission empire set up by the Labour Government's Transport Act of 1947. Yet its basic character and policy remained little altered.

Throughout his career, Rackham had been keen to foster standardisation in the more fundamental aspects of design across the entire AEC range — from 1930, for example, there had been one standard spring shackle pin covering all models. Even though the RT was visually and in many detail respects different from the 'provincial' Regent III, most of the major components were either alike or differed only in minor ways.

But in the early 1950s, this cohesive influence was lacking and there was something of a tug of war between London Transport's continuing drive towards fresh technological progress and elements at AEC which were themselves split between a rather conservative approach, a drive towards lightweight and basically simpler models and an interest in the low-floor concept for double-deckers.

In the event, Durrant's views largely prevailed on the Routemaster's design. However, the work of the Chiswick engineers in regard to brakes and suspension in particular must be acknowledged. Outstanding among these was Colin Curtis, whose career as a development engineer largely mirrored that of the model on which much of his work was concentrated.

Left:
Another unsuccessful but influential venture was AEC's underfloor-engined double-deck Regent IV prototype. This second body built for it by Park Royal and completed in June 1950 has a striking resemblance to the Routemaster design in the profile at the front of the upper deck as well as seating the same number of passengers, 64. No doubt the drawings were among those consulted when the Routemaster was being sketched out by LTE, Park Royal and AEC engineers.

CHAPTER TWO

THE PROTOTYPES

The basic design requirements for the new London Transport double-decker as visualised when serious work began in 1951 could be summed up as follows:

● An advance in terms of comfort and ease of driving on the RT.
● Suitability for trolleybus as well as bus replacement.
● A gain in operating economy, both in terms of fuel and other costs.

The increase in dimensions went some way to providing more comfort and also helped to allow a suitable compromise in terms of carrying capacity. The 7ft 6in limit had made it difficult to allow adequate shoulder width for passengers, especially at a time when more people wore heavy overcoats in winter and dressed in the expectation that there would be no heating in buses used on city services. Gangway room made it difficult for conductors to circulate freely to collect fares and standing passengers made movement inside the vehicle even more tedious. The extra 6in helped considerably and it was understandable that much of this was added to gangway width, though much of the problem had been the overlap of passengers unable to sit within the limitation of width provided by the seats themselves.

The 27ft length was not in itself enough to allow an extra row of seats as compared to the previous 26ft, but allowed what had been rather tight seat spacing to be made acceptable. In London, there was the precedent of the original version of the STL as built in 1932-33, seating 60 passengers within a body design with an almost vertical profile, which provided room for 34 seats on the top deck and 26 below. The vehicles in question had all been withdrawn by 1949, but the concept had fresh appeal in an era when buses were all too often full. The standard wartime lowbridge double-decker had seated 28 in the lower deck and so by adopting this figure it was only necessary to find room for another pair of seats on the top deck beyond the early STL version to produce a 64-seat double-decker. As mentioned in the last chapter, this total had been reached on the 1950 AEC Regent IV underfloor-engined prototype, but London Transport had not been attracted by the underfloor-engined concept.

It seems clear that this vehicle, especially in its Park Royal-bodied form, had quite a strong influence on the Routemaster's designers. The other unorthodox design which had clearly left its mark was the TF, with its curved-profile half-'bonnet'. Yet if an underfloor-engined double-decker was not acceptable, what else could be done to eliminate the conventional vertical radiator and also reduce bonnet length? The answer to this was the original Routemaster's most unorthodox feature in terms of layout and one that was not retained beyond the first prototype. There had been another intermediate step in attempting to combine the two features, this being a conversion carried out on one of the first production batch of RT-type buses, originally dating from 1940. This was RT97, which had been used as a basis for two experimental conversions beginning in 1945, when it had been modified to allow pay-as-you-enter operation, with seated conductor. This was a failure but the vehicle was subsequently used for a more extensive rebuild to become RTC1, a prototype for a projected breed of genuine double-deck Green Line coaches, as opposed to the thinly-disguised double-deck buses then in use on some busy routes.

The feature of RTC1 relevant to the Routemaster story was the removal of the standard radiator and its replacement by one mounted under the stairs, and forming part of an elaborate heating and ventilating system. The bonnet was reshaped to give an approximation to the TF profile, but in this case there was no attempt to reduce length. The vehicle was completed in this rebuilt form in January 1949 but by the end of the year it was taken off Green Line duty, having been found to be unsatisfactory, not least in being prone to overheating, and thus acting as a warning to later designers of unorthodox cooling systems, even if all too often unheeded.

However, the idea of a similarly-shaped front end clearly had strong appeal at Chiswick. There was also the thought that it should be possible to trim a useful slice off the length required for the engine and radiator installation. In this respect as well as others, the RT was a hard act to follow, for it was a model of compact design. Fitting a 9.6-litre six-cylinder in-line engine with a conventional radiator into a bonnet length of 4ft 6¼in took some beating. In the event, only 1½in was taken off this in the prototype Routemaster version, which used an underfloor radiator, though it has to be said that this aspect of the idea did not seem to have been pursued with much determination.

It was clearly more the other aspects of getting the radiator out of the way that held more fascination, notably achieving good low-angle vision for the driver and improving access to the engine. Not to be underrated was producing what was considered to be up-to-date appearance, for the tall-looking exposed radiator was out of fashion and in the early 1950s the bus industry seems to have been fascinated by the so-called 'new look' concept best publicised in the version evolved by Birmingham City Transport to which this name was particularly applied. London Transport had hitherto tended to set rather than follow fashion, but in this instance, there was at least a nod in its direction.

Now that the Routemaster is joining the company of traditional London institutions such as the Houses of Parliament, St Paul's Cathedral and the Yeomen of the Guard, there is apt to be a flavour of romanticism about its background. Recently the author heard part of a lyrical radio

talk in praise of the high standard of design of the Routemaster, extolling its subtle curves as well as practical merits. Much of it was music in his ears and it was good to hear public credit being given to 'some very distinguished old boys' at Chiswick for its advanced mechanical features — it was perhaps too much to expect the inclusion of those also involved at AEC and Park Royal — but a great deal was made of the part played by Douglas Scott, the industrial designer, who was commissioned to make a contribution to the vehicle's external and internal appearance. The impression was given that he was largely responsible for the overall form of the vehicle, but while his contribution must be acknowledged, his freedom to depart from the path laid down by previous designers was decidedly limited.

Except in the area of the radiator and bonnet, the family resemblance of the Routemaster to the RT, with a dash of the

The rebuild of the former RT97, one of the first production RT batch dating from 1940, as a double-deck Green Line coach prototype numbered RTC1 was completed in 1949. It was a failure in practical terms but pointed the way to later thinking and in particular the prototype Routemaster bonnet design.

Right:
The Routemaster prototype, RM1, in the form in which it made its first public appearance at the Commercial Motor Show in September-October 1954. Its frontal appearance was influenced by contemporary trends among other operators and manufacturers, though, the absence of a grille, apart from the six vertical slots below the bullseye motif, gave a 'different' look. It was decidedly controversial among bus enthusiasts but the public reacted more strongly to the paucity of destination display.

Park Royal Regent IV prototype already mentioned, is too strong to ignore. If a name should be mentioned, Eric Ottaway's influence was still strong for it was he who introduced the RT's flowing curves, though even they were a logical development of the STL body design as introduced in August 1934. Ottaway had been a senior member of the staff at Chiswick with the title Technical Officer, and thus basically an engineer with an artistic eye (in the honourable tradition of others before the 'school of art' type of industrial designer such as Douglas Scott tended to come to the fore).

The fourth and last of the pre-production prototypes was the Leyland-ECW Green Line coach, originally numbered CRL4 when it entered service in October 1957. By 1962, when seen here at Addlestone on the 716 route, it had become RMC4 to line up with the production Green Line version then entering service. *G. Rixon*

The main area of relative novelty in the Routemaster's external design was in the abandonment of the traditional exposed radiator and separate bonnet and front wings. Otherwise it was very much in the mould of its predecessors in general layout and other aspects of appearance. There was a remarkable degree of unanimity on double-deck vehicle layout among British bus operators in the first 10 years or so after World War 2. The combination of front-engined chassis and rear-entrance bodywork was standardised to an even greater extent than in the late prewar period by concerns of all categories and sizes and even such major users of double-deckers with entrance just behind the front axle in that period as Midland Red, Trent and the Country Bus department of London Transport had switched to the rear entrance. In fact, there were only two operators of any substance to favour the forward-entrance layout for double-deckers in the early postwar period — Barton Transport and Birch Bros, both independents.

So the Routemaster's conformity to this pattern is not so surprising as it may sometimes seem in retrospect — had its development come a little later, the picture might have been rather different. Certainly in London, the RT-type had laid down a standard of top-quality visual design, both in regard to the exterior and within the vehicle, that was hard to beat and indeed was still inspiring manufacturers elsewhere. Park Royal's own body designs for sale to provincial customers in the 1950-53 period were virtually to RT outline except in the cab and bulkhead area, while even Leyland was influenced by RT practice in details of interior finish of its standard own-make body for the Titan PD2/12 in the same period. Clearly, the Routemaster had to build on this reputation and the family resemblances were both the result of many of the same design team being involved and quite deliberate retention of the same principles of carefully considered form and proportions and attention to detail.

Considered in a little more analytical fashion, the Routemaster took most of the RT proportions as its basis, notably the four-bay structure (another feature which the RT had made quite fashionable and widely adopted by that date) and the mildly-rounded window outlines. The winding drop windows had proved popular with passengers and the decision to retain the same principle in the new bus, even though the depth of the opening portion was reduced, also

implied another item of continuity. In this respect, London was to remain out of line with convention elsewhere, for the top-sliding window was fast becoming almost universal outside the capital.

The more upright front-end was dictated by the increase in seating capacity and at the time seemed a little out of line with generally accepted practice, though it was to prove influential in the long run. At the rear, however, the RT had been somewhat unusual in its upright lines, the vertical outline carried up to upper-deck waist level giving a more severe profile than most of its contemporaries, or even its predecessors such as the standard London STL, though softened by the rear dome outline. The Routemaster was more akin to accepted contemporary practice in this respect, although oddly enough the rear view, with its smaller emergency exit window, now perhaps looks slightly more dated than that of the RT.

Yet if superficially orthodox by the standards of the period of its conception, the Routemaster was radically new under the skin, and even today, over a third of a century later, many of its features still seem advanced. Indeed, some have yet to be generally adopted and today's economic climate seems to have made one or two less likely to become accepted practice than was thought a decade or so ago. Reeled off in succession, the key features have quite a ring to them:

- Integral construction.
- Aluminium-alloy structure.
- Independent front suspension.
- Use of coil springs at both front and rear.
- Continuous-flow power hydraulic brake system.
- Direct-selection epicyclic gearbox.

A great deal of nonsense has been written about integral construction. As used in cars, it allowed both weight-saving and the production of a stiffer structure, exploiting the strength of relatively thin sheet steel when formed into the complex curves found for both practical and styling reasons in a modern car. A bus, by contrast, cannot help but be box-shaped in essential overall outline, give or take a little if highly desirable subtle shaping, and so the structure has to depend far more on its framework. Traditionally, and in many ways even nowadays, chassis were produced by firms whose traditions and skills concentrated on the mechanical side while the bodywork was the province of the coachbuilder, calling for a different type of expertise. The body always contributed much to the rigidity of the complete vehicle and when metal-framed could be counted as structural to an important extent.

It doubtless seemed a logical step to attach the mechanical units direct to the body and, indeed, London Transport had been involved in the development of trolleybuses built on this principle in the late 1930s. However, the underframe of such a vehicle had to be strong enough to take the stresses imposed by the suspension as well as heavy units carried by it, and inevitably was much more substantial than one designed to be supported on a chassis.

Although the Routemaster was integral in the sense of having no full-length chassis, it was fitted with what amounted to a 'half-chassis'. This carried the engine, front suspension, steering, driver's controls, etc in a manner very much the same as the front end of a conventional chassis. It had been standard practice ever since the beginning of forward-control buses for the cab and front of the upper deck to be self-supporting in the sense of being carried by the body front bulkhead and cantilevered from it. The Routemaster simply continued this principle but, in addition, there was what amounted to a sawn-off chassis frame extending back under the first bay of the body, so this, too, was cantilevered.

The epicyclic gearbox was carried directly by the body floor structure but the rear axle was attached to a pair of long radius arms pivoted to the floor framing just behind the gearbox and continued behind the axle to a cross-beam on the ends of which sat the rear coil springs. The upper ends of these were neatly accommodated under the rear end of the longitudinal seats just in front of the rear bulkhead. Strictly speaking, it was perhaps incorrect to describe this as a sub-frame, since it was directly connected to the body structure only at one end and sprung at the other, but on production vehicles it was ingeniously converted into the rear end of a 'chassis' when detached from the body shell at overhauls by being temporarily fastened to the front sub-frame. The mechanical units could thus be wheeled away for overhaul separately from the body in the manner long traditional within London Transport.

Integral construction is apt to be credited with weight reduction, but it seems clear that, in itself, the Routemaster's form of assembly could have contributed only marginally to the reduced weight which was, and still is, one of the model's most notable assets, particularly in view of the high standard of interior trim and seat comfort. So what was the secret? The use of an almost wholly aluminium structure played a key role in this, with both the framing and panelling almost entirely in this light material. The first prototype turned the scales at 6ton 14cwt 2qr unladen, unusually light for a 27ft-long 8ft-wide double-decker and more the sort of figure associated with a 26ft by 7ft 6in bus of the 1937-39 period, when weight had to be kept down to a figure of about this level to keep within the gross laden weight limit of those days if 56 seated passengers were to be carried. There had been lighter buses to the 27ft by 8ft dimensions, but almost without exception, they had what can only be called skimpy specification and interior trim and in some cases construction bordering on the flimsy.

Below:
Removing the radiator from its 'obvious' position in front of the engine made it easier to adopt a rounded profile for the bonnet of the Routemaster prototype. Removal of the detachable front panel gave reasonable access to the 9.6-litre AEC engine, basically the same unit as that of the RT. This photograph was dated 25 September 1954.
W. H. R. Godwin

Right:
Seen in Surbiton on 9 May 1962, the first day of Routemaster operation of the new 281 route, replacing the oldest London trolleybus route 601, which was among the final routes to run for the last time the previous day, is RM1114. The trolleybus overhead wires had yet to be removed. *G. Rixon*

Far right:
Routemaster production was in full swing in July 1962, when both standard red Routemasters, including RM1286 in the foreground, and some of the Green Line batch then being built, including RMC1460, are prominent among the vehicles passing through AEC's inspection shop, itself quite new at the time. Just visible on the right of the picture is an Eastbourne Corporation Regent V. *G. Rixon*

Far right:
RMF1254 proved to be a prototype not for London Transport's later Routemasters but for the sole customer for the model outside LTE or its influence. Northern General Transport's order for 50 Routemasters with Leyland O.600 engines caused widespread interest. Number 2117, seen here, was one of the second delivery, dating from January 1965. It is seen in original livery in July 1973 but with the grey-painted wheels by then being adopted as part of the corporate livery of National Bus Company subsidiaries, NGT having by then passed into that group.
G. P. B. Martin

Right:
In the summer of 1965, the RML was adopted as the standard for London Transport's last bulk order for 500 Routemasters. The 10th vehicle numerically was RML2270, but its new-looking appearance in this view was the result of a 'glossy'-style overhaul of the type being applied to selected vehicles by the early 1980s. It is seen here at Hyde Park Corner on the 137 route on 18 August 1981.
G. Rixon

smoke from both homes, still mostly burning coal, and industry with atmospheric fog.

RM1 was officially taken into LTE stock in September 1954 but did not enter service until February 1956, the intervening time being taken up by testing and further development, which included spells at both Chobham and Nuneaton, where test track work was carried out. Meanwhile, early in 1955, RM2 was completed, being outwardly generally similar to RM1 apart from the provision of a more conventional front panel with a grille for the radiator placed in a more conventional position. This was possible within the still current 27ft length because at that stage it was fitted with an engine of the AV470 type as used in the lightweight version of the Regent V. This was of 7.75-litre capacity and hence more compact than the 9.6-litre unit, and was quoted as having an output of 112bhp in some contemporary literature, though the Regent application was quoted at 103bhp.

It is not difficult to detect the LTE engineers' lack of enthusiasm for the return to an engine size reminiscent of that used in the prewar STL. More promising were two other aspects of advances in design first seen on that vehicle, the fully-automatic transmission and power-assisted steering.

The gearbox was basically similar to the version in RM1, but gear changes were made automatically in response to speed and, at first, accelerator pressure. With the combination of hydraulically-operated brakes and power steering using a similar medium a hydraulically-operated gearbox not only made good sense in standardising the systems on the vehicle, with some simplification of items required but had been found to give smoother and more consistent gear-changes. Unfortunately, AEC was committed to making air-operated epicyclic gearboxes for its passenger models for other customers and was not prepared to put a hydraulic unit into production, so production Routemasters had a rather curious set-up, with air compressor, reservoir and piping for gearbox operation, as well as the hydraulic pump and related items for the brakes and steering.

Other development was in hand, and a feature criticised on the first prototype, the smaller than standard front destination display, was replaced by a three-panel unit of similar pattern though different layout to the RT standard and the side box was also enlarged. A heating and ventilating system had also been added, a feature which at that date was still uncommon on a British city bus. The weight had crept up in consequence to 6ton 17cwt. RM1 entered service for the first time while in this form on 8 February 1956 on Route 2 between Golders Green and Crystal Palace. It had the appropriate-seeming registration number SLT 56 and in due course the other prototypes appeared with the succeeding numbers SLT 57-59.

In addition to RM2, there were to be two further prototypes. Leyland was in those days AEC's main competitor, even though there was some co-operation between the two firms in railcars and what little was left in the line of trolleybus business. London Transport's management was conscious of the implications of monopolies even though its history had established the close link with AEC and it was thought prudent as well as technologically useful to produce versions with Leyland O.600 engines and Pneumocyclic gearboxes, the former being the 9.8-litre unit already familiar in London in the RTL and RTW buses and the latter the Leyland equivalent to the AEC-build direct-selection or automatic gearbox, incidentally christened Monocontrol for AEC sales purposes. The body shell of RML3, as it was to be called, was put in hand at Weymann's, which had been Park Royal's 'partner', though again a competitor, in building most of the RT bodies.

The fourth vehicle was to be bodied by Eastern Coach Works, at that time a wholly-owned subsidiary of the British Transport Commission and supplier of almost all the bodywork needs of the Tilling group which continued to constitute the BTC company bus operations in England and Wales. It was restricted by a clause in the Transport Act 1947 to building for state-owned organisations and had capacity to meet more than just the Tilling needs, so could have supplied at least part of LTE's needs. All four prototypes had a great deal in common covering both their mechanical and body design. However, they were used to explore alternative ideas, not only such things as the possible use of Leyland as opposed to AEC engines but also specification variations.

The fourth prototype was to be a Green Line coach, for example, and was thus CRL4, having more comfortable seats for 57 passengers, platform doors and net-type parcel racks. It was also fitted with a different type of front suspension, using torsion bars instead of coil springs but this was to remain peculiar to this vehicle. Both the two Leyland-engined buses were under construction in July 1956 when the length limit for double-deck two-axle buses was increased to 30ft and this helped to resolve the problem of reconciling the preference for a relatively generous engine size with the original amount of body space without the need to adopt the unsatisfactory underfloor radiator system.

The idea of building to take full advantage of the increase in permitted length did not yet appeal and in this LTE was not alone, quite a number of operators continuing to specify double-deckers of about 27ft overall. For the RM, however, only a few extra inches were added, RM1 being rebuilt with front radiator and the length increased to 27ft 4in almost as soon as this became allowable, power-assisted steering also being fitted at this stage. RM2 was also fitted with a 9.6-litre engine after trials. It had run in primer during initial tests but was finished in country area green and cream, entering service from Reigate on 20 May 1957 on Route 406. However, its stay there was brief and it was repainted red and was transferred to Turnham Green, very near Chiswick and often a home for experimental vehicles, in September of that year.

Meanwhile, the two Leyland-powered prototypes were making progress. RML3 was completed at Weymann towards the end of 1956, thus being the first Routemaster built up outside Chiswick, and was officially taken into LTE stock in July 1957. By that time CRL4 was completed and entered service from Romford on Route 721 in October 1957, by then having a 55-seat capacity and being fitted with a semi-automatic version of the gearbox. Both of these vehicles had a different design of bonnet to that of RM1 and 2, with the raised portion over the engine reduced in width and the nearside wing treatment reverting to something nearer the RT style. The protruding panel carrying the radiator grille was rather obviously an afterthought on all four prototypes at this stage and the appearance was somewhat 'bitty'. The final one to enter service was RML3, from Willesden garage on Route 8, in January 1958.

Far left:
The country bus department's turn for Routemasters came in the winter of 1965-66, when two batches of RML-types were the first new double-deckers to be added to the fleet since the RT era, save for the brief appearance of prototype RM2 in 1957. By the time this view of RML2428 was taken in Uxbridge on 18 June 1978, it had long been in the ownership of London Country Bus Services Ltd, but still bore the LTE shade of dark green, albeit with the yellow relief favoured by LCBS in its early days. *G. Rixon*

Left:
The final batch of Routemasters to be built consisted of more red RML buses. By a quirk of circumstance, they received registration marks NML with E suffix and SMK with F, both of which would have denoted Middlesex until 1967, when that county's marks were merged with others in a common series covering Greater London. A Middlesex registration on an AEC bus had usually signified a former demonstrator, so the AEC connection with London double-deckers was oddly highlighted at its end. RML2744, a little battered but with shiny paint, is seen at Stonebridge Park in October 1978. *G. Rixon*

CHAPTER THREE

PRODUCTION

The prototype development programme was by no means complete when London Transport announced the placing of the first bulk order, in October 1956. Only RM1 had reached the stage of having been in public service and even it had then been withdrawn for conversion to the front-radiator form, while RM2 was still involved in experimental running and the two Leyland versions had yet to be completed. Yet the placing

of the order for 850 buses to be produced by AEC and Park Royal was by no means a foregone conclusion.

Lord Black, who had been associated with Park Royal since 1934 (when as W. R. Black he had joined the firm as director and general manager) and AEC since the two firms became associated in 1949 – he was about to become managing director of the ACV group to which both firms belonged – told the author that the price was cut to the bone to secure the order. Clearly, this was logical in the sense that further orders could be expected and the development costs thereby spread over the total output. Yet the possibility that Leyland and Metro-Cammell Weymann (the sales company which acted for both Metro-Cammel and Weymann), in those days working together on a number of projects, might secure the order was seen as a genuine threat. The rivalry between Leyland and AEC was intense and Donald, later Lord, Stokes was highly successful in securing bus orders from major operators at home and abroad for Leyland.

Even so, the continuity with LTE, AEC and Park Royal as partners in the Routemaster project was logical in view of the work done. The 850 vehicles were intended as a first stage in the task of replacing London Transport's fleet of 1,500 trolleybuses, most of which dated from the period betwen 1935 and 1941, with only 127 dating from later than 1947. Delivery was scheduled to begin in 1958 but in the event the trolleybus replacement programme was able to begin by using surplus existing buses. Some of the last batches of RT-type buses had been stored rather than placed in service in 1954, and further cuts in service as demand for bus travel dropped meant that more buses were available despite the fact that the double-deck bus fleet was entirely of RT or closely related types and dated from 1947 or later.

The basic specification for the production vehicles was, in effect, that of RM1 as built plus the features subsequently added, principally fully-automatic transmission, power-assisted steering and the heating and ventilating system but minus the underfloor radiator. It is noteworthy that there was no attempt to lower standards for passengers or driver as had been adopted by some makers and operators in an effort to reduce weight and hence operating costs. This was noteworthy, as LTE was under increasing financial pressure. Weight reduction had been kept as a high priority throughout, of course, but the temptation to remove perhaps another half ton by stripping out interior trim and fitting less comfortable seats had been resisted. In fact weight had risen and the standard production 64-seat Routemaster carried lettering showing the unladen weight as 7ton 5cwt – in the usual London Transport way the figure was rounded off and no doubt individual vehicles varied by 2-3cwt, as was shown up by Leyland's practice of individual weighing. This was, and

still is a very creditable figure, for it was 5cwt less than the RT despite being approximately 1ft 6in longer, 6in wider and having seats for eight more passengers, while the durability is now shown to be even greater (though the RT's life could well have been extended had it been desirable on economic grounds).

The external appearance of the production Routemaster was improved by a new shape of bonnet and wing assembly, the bonnet top tapering downwards more noticeably and the radiator grille creeping back a little nearer to the AEC shape so long associated with London buses though at that stage still lacking the triangle badge. The various parts fitted together more neatly but to this observer the projection of the grille and headlamp panels beyond the cab front lost the neat effect given by the smoother profile of the RT. The general appearance of the body had changed little from that of the prototype as originally built apart from changes associated with the heating and ventilating system and minor revisions to light units. Perhaps understandably, the Chiswick engineers thought that the provision of ducted ventilation would allow the elimination of the drop windows at the front of the upper deck, a traditional London bus feature almost as old-

Left:
The operational career of FRM1 was, understandably, somewhat erratic. Various teething troubles were experienced, and the bus tended to be out of use for long periods, particularly when parts not common to other models were needed. It is seen in Parliament Square on 5 September 1981 during the period when it was based at Stockwell garage for sightseeing tour duties. *G. Rixon*

Right:
The scene in Mortlake garage on Sunday, 10 December 1978 is one that could have been reproduced in many London garages at almost any time over the last quarter of a century or more, give or take a few details. Nearest the camera is RM1207, with most of the other vehicles identifiable belonging to the batch with reversed CLT registrations dating from 1961-63. Visible in the background is a preserved RT in pre-1950 livery and one of the ex-London Country Routemasters, temporarily stored pending a decision as to its future. *G. Rixon*

established as the covered top double-decker itself, yet one rarely found elsewhere in Britain. The RM prototypes had lost them and so did production buses until adverse public reaction brought them back from RM251.

The standard engine for the production vehicles was the AEC AV590 unit, having the same 9.6-litre swept volume and 120mm by 142mm bore and stroke dimensions as the A204 unit used in the standard RT, but of the form of construction used in the smaller AV470 engine that had been tried in RM2. This used 'wet' cylinder liners – in other words, the cylinder barrels in which the pistons operated were in direct contact with the cooling water for most of their length, and being readily detachable when the engine was dismantled, had to be adequately sealed at top and bottom to prevent water leaks. The cylinder block and crankcase, separate parts in the RT version, were now in one casting, a form of construction sometimes described as monobloc and a feature shared with the Leyland O.600, though that had the 'dry' type of cylinder liners inserted into full-depth cylinder bores, as used on the older AEC units, such as the A204.

The AV590 engines could thus be said to be directly equivalent to the older types of 9.6-litre engine in their capabilities, though for some applications the power output was higher, simply in the course of development common to later versions of most engine types. The difference in construction, and in particular the wet-liner system, was to prove troublesome in some applications, usually where maximum power was called upon for lengthy periods. This did not prove to be a major problem with the Routemaster, probably because of its modest weight and London Transport's decision to retain the conservative 115bhp power output, as well as London's mainly level or gently undulating terrain and the easy timing of most routes. Thus the AV590 remained standard for the main Routemaster types throughout the period of production – other AEC models switched to the subsequent AV691 engine from 1966 so far as catalogue listings were concerned, but the standard Routemaster RM and RML models stayed with the AV590 to the end of manufacture early in 1968.

The first production bus to be completed was RM8, exhibited on the Park Royal stand at the 1958 Commercial Motor Show, the numbers RM5 to 7 being left blank temporarily, evidently because the first three sets of mechanical units had been assembled for test purposes, two being under temporary lorry-like vehicles to build up mileage under service conditions as quickly as possible. As it turned out those units were fitted to later body shells and the relation of the various serial numbers became decidedly confused. The four prototypes were given 'chassis' numbers which were the same as their fleet numbers, RM1 being chassis RM1 and so on. For production, AEC began a series of numbers in line with its coded system of the time, beginning at R2RH001, one of the test sets, which later went under RM459, the 'R' standing for Routemaster, '2' for two-pedal (ie no clutch pedal) transmission, 'R' for right-hand steering and 'H' for hydraulic brake system. London Transport's own type coding system gave the code 5RM5 to the standard production Routemaster, this signifying the marriage of 5RM 'chassis' with RM5 body, the codes 1RM1 to 4RM4 having been given to the prototypes in sequence. Also in usual LTE fashion, the basic code was subdivided in the manner 2/5RM5/2 to signify minor variations. On earlier types, these subdivisions sometimes covered quite significant features but on the Routemaster they were used to distinguish alternative makes of minor equipment, basically electrical but including the automatic gearbox control unit. Their function in this case was to identify items which had to be matched on the chassis units and the body.

In particular, the 5RM5 code does not respond to the most obvious item which distinguished some of the standard 64-seat Routemasters from the rest – the Leyland O.600 engine option. London Transport engineers preferred not to have all their eggs in one basket, and although Leyland did not get in on the main contracts for the Routemaster, it was a deliberate decision to include a proportion of Leyland-engined buses in the new fleet, just as had applied to the RT family (though in that case Leyland supplied the complete chassis with only a small proportion of AEC-built components). Curiously, though, there was a certain lack of enthusiasm for the result. The standard Leyland double-deckers using the O.600, the Titan PD2 and PD3, are widely agreed to have been among the all-time greats of bus design. Yet the LTE was never all that enthusiastic about its RTL or, despite their 8ft width, RTW buses and the Leyland-powered Routemasters were much the same.

Be that as it may, the resulting vehicle was manifestly 'different' and it seemed illogical to code it 5RM5 and hence anyone with the kind of mind that likes to put labels on variations is better served by AEC, which kindly designated the sets of chassis units with Leyland engine 2R2RH. As built, the production Leyland-engined Routemasters were RM632, RM870, RM1009, RM1255-1452, RM1521-1719 and RM1811-1986, but on overhaul these engines did not necessarily return to buses within these batches of numbers and the 626 engines involved could latterly more safely be identified by the different, rather harsher, noise they made.

The original order for 850 production buses was increased to 1,150 before completion and, in practice, the vehicles which entered service tended to be split up into batches as variations were introduced. Air suspension was for a time a case in point, having been tried for the rear axle of RM2 and CRL4 during the prototype programme and also on RM8. A further 50 sets were ordered and fitted to RM75 and RM87-135, even this stage of the exercise being split into some four varieties as the object was to gain experience of alternative types. Both Dunlop and Firestone were involved as equipment suppliers and each produced main sets of units for 20 vehicles, of the Dunlop Pneuride and Firestone Airide types respectively, but there were also five Dunlop Dillow and five Firestone Airide of an alternative version with slower and hence softer-seeming frequency. An advantage of air suspension was the constant ride height, valuable on a rear-entrance bus on which rear-suspension deflection is magnified by the positioning of the platform in the rear overhang of the vehicle. However, after a three-year trial, it was decided against further development and the buses were fitted with the coil-spring suspension as used on other Routemasters, itself giving a noticeably better standard of ride than the then conventional leaf springs.

More significant was the development of a longer Routemaster. As has already been mentioned, the legal limit on overall length for a two-axle double-decker was increased from 27ft to 30ft in 1956. Most models offered by the various makers were modified to take advantage of this, some being in production within a few months. By no means all operators wanted to make the change, however, some arguing that a 27ft bus provided the seating capacity suitable to their needs while others were inhibited by trade union attitudes. The latter had powerful impact, and the attitude of the Transport & General

Facing page, top:
Front sub-frame units in the works yard at Park Royal awaiting assembly into Routemasters. They incorporated the AV590 engines with fluid flywheels and indeed almost all of the front-end mechanical content of the vehicle, including the independent front suspension and driving controls other than the steering wheel, removed for safe keeping. The temporary support at the rear was designed to keep the unit level.

Facing page, bottom:
The rear axle sub-assemblies were stacked up, not being fitted with wheels or the coil springs located at each end of the cross-member until fitted to the body structure.

Far left:
Year-round bus operation inevitably exposes vehicles to wintry weather and, perhaps more significant, the salt used to combat snow and ice. The Routemaster's aluminium-alloy structure has proved much more resistant to corrosion than most steel-framed body designs. Seen in Richmond in December 1981 is RM1179. *G. Rixon*

Centre:
This pair of pictures show another former Green Line in successive liveries. In this view, RCL2249 is seen still on Green Line duties on the 716 to Woking early in 1978, painted in NBC green. By August 1980, the same vehicle had been repainted red after transfer to the LTE fleet and is seen on the 149 with bus-type headlamps, looking almost immaculate apart from some scratches on the front roof dome. *G. Rixon*

Left:
This view of KGJ 612D shows the trailer which formed an essential part of the package, for luggage space on the vehicle itself would have been hopelessly inadequate for all but small items of baggage. Dating from March 1978, the picture shows the vehicle at Heathrow and reveals the rather grubby look when the cream paintwork became soiled. *G. Rixon*

Right:
The possibilities of a longer Routemaster were explored by a batch of 24, the vehicle show here being the first, delivered as ER880 in July 1961, but renumbered as shown to RML880 before entering service in November. The extra length was produced by inserting a 2ft 2in bay in the middle of the structure, giving an appearance which lost a little of the tidy look of the standard model but helped to maintain standardisation of most body parts.

Workers Union, the largest in the bus industry, was one of opposition to larger buses although in due time some sort of deal was struck. There was also the suitability of bigger buses for operation in heavy traffic when the nimble characteristics of a manoeuvrable vehicle could be valuable, especially in London.

On the other hand the ability to increase seating capacity to 72 had obvious appeal, and the experience of other operators who had adopted bigger buses had shown that city operation was quite practical. The integral construction and use of standardised modules in the Routemaster led to the decision to simply add a short bay in the middle of the structure. While this gave rather a makeshift look to the completed vehicle, it had the practical advantage of retaining standard components for such items as opening windows. The two sub-frames with the mechanical components were almost unaltered, apart from the increased propeller shaft length and tyres to suit the heavier vehicle and accordingly were classified as R2RH/1 by AEC – curiously, AEC's practice in this respect was rather reminiscent of older Chiswick practice. London Transport, however, preferred to keep things tidy and used the code 7RM7 for the 30ft version, giving the clue that another variant had already been 'spoken for'. The extra length of 2ft 4in applied both to the wheelbase, which thus went up from the 16ft 10in of the standard RM to 19ft 2in, and the overall length from the 27ft 6½in of the standard production RM to 29ft 10½in.

The extra length allowed an extra row of four seats on each deck, making the seating capacity 40 on the top and 32 below. The increase in weight was 10cwt, which made the longer version more efficient in terms of weight per passenger than the standard one. London Transport's long-standing preference for using the same 9.00-20 tyre size at both front and rear which had been maintained from pre-war days through the RT and standard RM finally had to go, the front tyres now being 10.00-20 – still a smaller size than that used on standard AEC 27ft and indeed almost any other double-decker model's front wheels.

At first, the fleet number prefix letters chosen for the longer model were ER – Extended Routemaster – but this was only applied to ER880-882 before it was decided that RML would be a better choice and the whole initial batch of 24 vehicles entered service as RML880-903 in the winter of 1961-62. They were regarded as experimental to some degree, and it was not until 1965 and what was to prove the final stages of the Routemaster programme that the RML was adopted as the standard production bus version. The Leyland-engined prototype RML3 was renumbered simply as RM3.

The trolleybus replacement programme was nearing its end by this time and of the 14 stages in which it was carried out, all but the first three, completed in 1959, used Routemaster buses, and in turn all of these, but for the 24 RML buses allocated to replace the 609 trolleybuses which ran up the Finchley Road, were 64-seat buses. Declining numbers of passengers were making the reduced capacity as compared to 70-seat trolleybuses less important than had been thought but with the final conversion in May 1962, the question of replacing time-expired buses came back into the picture. Virtually the whole London double-deck motorbus fleet was composed of 56-seaters and as the RT fleet approached the stage when its older members were reaching their 15th birthdays, continued Routemaster production fitted logically. In fact, quite a number of both the RT and RTL types had already been sold due to the fall-off in traffic rendering the LTE fleet larger than was needed, but what was in mind when decisions on future orders were being taken was more of a normal fleet renewal programme.

At that time, London Transport was already facing growing financial and, to some degree, political problems. A six-week strike in the summer of 1958 had produced a permanent drop in passenger traffic in addition to the normal-seeming steady decline due to increasing use of cars and greater readiness of people to stay at home in the evenings as television became more popular. It seemed logical to propose a replacement programme based on the principle of putting 10 Routemasters on the road to take over from 11 RTs, which would have given a useful cut in operating costs and yet not reduced the passenger-carrying capacity per hour as the buses passed any given point on the route. The widening of headway at a time when many routes still had very frequent services would hardly have been catastrophic but the trade union would have none of it. At that date, its power was still immense and although negotiations dragged on for a time, by the end of 1962

Above:
The first of the production Routemaster coaches, RMC1453, is seen when posed for an official photograph and handing-over ceremony in the Park Royal works yard in June 1962. *AEC*

Far left:
Routemasters with all over advertising were often very different from standard in colours but RM1237 was in a style not too far removed from standard when celebrating 200 years of the toothbrush for the Wisdom concern. It was seen at Trafalgar Square on 8 June 1980. *G. Rixon*

Left:
More typical of the species was RML2492, advertising Underwood's photographic printing service when seen on 10 June 1984. *G. Rixon*

LT had conceded that replacement would be on a one-for-one basis. This being so, the case for the bigger bus was weakened and the 64-seater continued to be the standard.

By the end of 1962, deliveries had reached RM1382 and the production programme up to the end of 1964 took planned deliveries up to RM2156, roundly 1,000 more buses having been added to the original expanded initial bulk order. In practice, the picture was again rather more complex and indeed vehicles already in existence added to the growing variety of variants. The 6RM6 code, hitherto missing, was filled in by the RMC class, the production coach version of the standard 'short' RM, which entered Green Line service in the summer of 1962. This had the general character of the prototype CRL4 translated to the standard AEC-Park Royal product. Seating was for 57 passengers, with 32 upstairs and 25 down, retaining longitudinal seats over the rear wheel arches rather than the individual angled seats tried out on the prototype. The seats themselves were of similar style to the standard version, with

double top rail, but were more deeply upholstered and more generously spaced.

Outwardly, the RMC was distinguished by its platform doors, quadruple headlights, different destination display and, of course, the Green Line livery, in those days a dignified two-tone green with the relief in light green applied to strips surrounding the windows as well as the between-decks band. There were quite a number of less obvious differences, such as air suspension for the rear axle, higher gearing, with 4.7 to 1 rear axle ratio in place of the standard 5.22 to 1, semi-automatic control for the gearbox instead of the usual fully automatic system, greater fuel capacity and interior luggage racks. The batch consisted of 68 vehicles, numbered RMC1453-1520, entering service on a series of routes where the contemporary standard RF-type single-deckers were of inadequate capacity. There had been operation of some Green Line routes by double-deckers since wartime, but these had been run by standard buses of various types, latterly RT models with little more than livery differences from the bus versions. The additional features of the RMC put the unladen weight up to 7ton 15cwt, making them as heavy as the RML.

Although bearing a considerably lower number, the next Routemaster variant to appear, RMF1254, was not revealed to the world at large until the Commerical Motor Show in October 1962. This was a 30ft (or to be precise, 29ft 10½in) version using the RML-type pillar spacing and 19ft 2in wheelbase, but with forward-entrance layout. This last-mentioned feature had come into quite widespread favour among company bus fleets from the late 1950s but had not been seen on a London Transport design since the final batch of Country Area STL buses of this layout had entered service in 1936. It never caught on in a big way among British urban operators, the only major city municipal undertaking to adopt it on a fairly large scale at the beginning of the 1960s being Glasgow.

It thus always seemed a fairly unlikely bet as a pointer to future London bus development, but was to have useful spin-offs in terms of Routemaster production. As built, RMF1254 seated 69, with 38 on top and 31 below, and here again it compared poorly with the 72 of the RML, though there was a very slight weight saving, this bus weighing 7tons 14cwt. This was slightly surprising in view of the provision of power-operated doors, but evidently other features compensated for this. The trade union reaction was one of suspicion to any increase in seating capacity and the 24 RML buses had probably only got by because they replaced trolleybuses of almost equal capacity. London Transport went through its usual process of issuing a type code – 1/7RM8 – but somehow the whole project had a slight air of unreality, as if it was not taken all that seriously. It was noteworthy that no side destination indicator was provided, and although it could be argued that the proximity of the entrance to the front of the vehicle made one less necessary, it was another item which suggested that perhaps its purpose was not primarily a prototype for future London service.

A more important clue lay in the revised radiator grille, with the triangular radiator badge that had been associated with AEC buses since 1929 restored to what many would think its rightful place at the top. Although the badge itself carried London Transport lettering, as had been so on AEC buses built for LT service since 1934, it was, to traditionalists (among whom the author confesses to belonging) even more 'AEC-flavoured' than contemporary products of the Southall factory destined for other customers, for the grille outline bore a close resemblance to what had been the AEC style of what could be called the Rackham era. In fact, there had been a much belated realisation that the Routemaster did have potential for a wider market.

Just why no direct attempt had been made to sell the model to other customers in the period up to 1962 is a matter for speculation. There was a lack of clear-cut policy on double-deckers at AEC in the early and mid-1950s, with continuation of the conventional Regent chassis and development of a low-floor integral-construction model, the Bridgemaster, taking place alongside the Routemaster prototype work. The fact that London Transport was overstocked with modern double-deckers and would not need new vehicles in any large numbers for several years did not help in encouraging the choice of any programme based on London production as its core in the way that had applied during the RT and indeed previous periods. Moreover, the mood of many operators outside London was one of looking for more basic models with low running costs and the 'fancy' Routemaster was a good deal too elaborate for such tastes. On the other hand, the Bridgemaster had remarkably little in common with the Routemaster beyond its name, the use of integral construction and independent front suspension and

the opportunity of spreading costs over the two ranges by using common parts seems to have been missed in a way which one cannot help thinking would not have happened in the Rackham era.

Be that as it may, the Routemaster was clearly on the back burner until 1958, as far as a model to go into regular production was concerned. The Bridgemaster never fulfilled its expectations, partly due to problems of its association with the Crossley works and the decision to close those premises, but largely because the British Electric Traction group at which it was largely aimed had only a limited interest in low-height double-deckers. Yet by 1962, the Bridgemaster had given way to another low-floor double-deck project, this time a chassis with conventional front axle, reviving the Renown name.

Left:
When the author became full-time Editor of *Buses Illustrated* in 1963, it was published from Ian Allan's then offices at Craven House, Hampton Court, this view of RMC1509 being taken from the window. With his home then in East Barnet, it proved possible to travel home almost all the way on the 716 route, the journey time being much the same as when travelling by train into London and onward by tube – the RMC won hands down in terms of comfort! *Ian Allan Library*

Right:
A feature of London buses in the later LTE era was the use of buses in official special liveries to mark events or anniversaries. When the 150th anniversary of Shillibeer's pioneer horsebus service was approaching, RM2, by then almost standard in frontal appearance, was painted in this style to try out the idea – it was meant to resemble that of Shillibeer's vehicle which brought the word 'omnibus' as a description of a public vehicle into the language. It is seen at the Syon Park gala on 17 September 1978 but did not enter service in this livery. *G. Rixon*

Yet the climate of opinion in terms of double-deck design was altering in some ways. Through the mid- and late-1950s, Leyland was developing its Atlantean rear-engined double-decker, attracting sizeable orders on its appearance in production form in 1958, and inspiring Daimler to follow suit, though going one better in terms of specification with low-floor capability, with the Fleetline from 1960. Such vehicles were inevitably more complex and there was also increasing acceptance that driving a large bus in city traffic was becoming increasingly difficult in itself, justifying such aids to the driver as semi- if not fully-automatic transmission.

Curiously enough, the growth of interest in the idea of at least investigating the potential provincial market for the Routemaster almost coincided with the takeover – officially 'merger' – of AEC by Leyland. It would be quite misleading to deduce that either the announcement of the Renown or the more discreet and still decidedly cautious promotion of the Routemaster as a model that might be made generally available was anything to do with the merger. In truth, the Leyland influence was to kill off what might have been the most promising Routemaster project of all. But the merger announcement in June 1962 was followed by the appearance of RMF1254 at the Earls Court Show in October, not in itself out of line with what had gone before of course, since there had been Routemaster exhibits from the start, but more significantly a series of demonstration visits followed.

It was Liverpool Corporation that put RMF1254 into public service almost immediately after the Show, although as that undertaking was on the point of taking delivery of the first of 200 Leyland Atlantean buses it is hardly surprising that no order ensued. Liverpool had long been an AEC stronghold but the arrival of a standard Routemaster, RM1414, in Manchester Corporation service for two weeks in February 1963 was more of a surprise, though this was a Leyland-engined bus. Then RMF1254 moved to the East Kent company, which at that time was standardising on 30ft AEC Regent V models with forward-entrance Park Royal bodywork, suggesting some affinity in thought though these were synchromesh-gearbox buses and EK remained faithful to that concept until virtually the end of Routemaster production in 1967. However, it may well have been this visit that led to the only sales of Routemasters to an operator other than in London.

Both East Kent and Northern General Transport were companies in the British Electric Traction group, and although that organisation allowed individual concern a fair degree of freedom of action in such matters as the choice and specification of vehicles, it had a well-organised and active organisation for assessing the merits of potential models or other products. Without doubt, information on the experience obtained would be available within the group. At that period, NGT was standardised largely on Leyland for its double-deckers, though it had long also been an AEC user. Many of its routes were of a highly-intensive urban character, serving the largely built-up areas of Tyneside and Wearside, but it also ran on a series of inter-urban routes running across County Durham and of lengths up to about 30 miles. Several were operated jointly with United Automobile Services, running as

they did for what were often quite a considerable part of their mileage in that company's territory. As a Tilling company, UAS standardised on the Bristol Lodekka for double-deck requirements and on these routes was using the FLF 30ft forward-entrance model with air suspension on the rear axle.

There had long been a sense of rivalry between NGT and UAS and so there was an element of company pride involved. It seems that the Leyland Atlantean with decidedly spartan interior of the early designs of MCW or Park Royal/Roe bodywork was not considered appropriate, and it may also be that the reliability problems of early versions of this model were beginning to have an effect on new vehicle order decisions – several BET companies turned away from the Atlantean for a time around this period. So NGT decided on an order for Routemasters to a specification based on that of RMF1254, but with Leyland O.600 engines, semi-automatic rather than fully-automatic gearboxes and worm-drive rear axles, the last-mentioned feature reflecting traditional British practice for such units had been standard for most British front-engined double-deckers since the original Leyland Titan, the standard Routemaster and, indeed, the Atlantean being among the first to break with that tradition. They also had 72-seat capacity, the additional three going on the upper deck, and top-sliding windows, two on each side of each deck, were deemed more suitable for the rigours of the chillier climate of northeastern England.

A total of 50 buses were ordered, but they were split into two batches, the first 18 following the LT batches which took the RM series of fleet numbers to RM2160, in terms of chassis number series, and being delivered in the spring of 1984. The remaining 32 followed quite soon after, beginning in October of that year, though delivery was spread into the following year and the last did not enter service until June 1965. They had chassis numbers which fitted between those of RML2598 and 2599, though as was often the case with AEC chassis numbers this was misleading in the sense that the latter London Transport vehicles were not built until 1966.

During all this time, RMF1254 had never entered service in London, though it made another demonstration visit, to Halifax in October 1963. In his usual fashion, Geoffrey Hilditch, then General Manager of that municipal undertaking, wrote frankly in the August 1965 issue of *Bus & Coach* of his findings on this and several other makes and models during a

series of trials that were carried out at that time. The Routemaster scored high marks for suspension and stability – he reckoned that corners could be negotiated at speeds impossible in any conventional model – and also for ease of maintenance, scoring top marks in a series of tests on the accessibility of servicing points and ease of unit changes. Clearly, the model's operator-bred background lay behind this, but the price was evidently a factor which influenced the decision on future orders away from the model – Halifax eventually settled on the Daimler Fleetline after a brief flirtation with the Dennis Loline.

Meanwhile, not only was Routemaster output for London continuing steadily but further developments were afoot. Standard Routemasters licensed had reached RM2105 by the end of 1964. Somewhat ironically, the merger of AEC with

Above:
The RCL could be described as a cross between the RMC and the RML, with the latter's 'half-bay' amidships and the quadruple headlamps and other characteristics of the former. The last of the type, RCL2260, is seen in a Park Royal official photograph before delivery.

Far left:
The wedding of the Prince of Wales was the occasion for another set of specially-painted RMs, this time numbering eight for service plus a prototype. Seen here on the Royal Wedding special service on Tuesday 28 July 1981 is RM219.
G. Rixon

Left:
Another anniversary was the half-century of London Transport, and RM1933 is seen in appropriate 1933 livery at Pimlico on Route 24 on 18 August 1983. Strictly speaking, London Transport had at first continued the use of the General fleetname, but history was, for once, to repeat itself with the revival of the London General Omnibus Co title for one of the localised subsidiaries of London Buses in 1989, with some vehicles in the complete General style.
G. Rixon

Leyland had contributed to the end of manufacture of Leyland-engined versions for London service as one of the main justifications – the use of an alternative supplier – had vanished when the hitherto competitive firms came together. However, the production of the hitherto standard 27ft rear-entrance version of the model was almost at an end, for RM2217, delivered in April 1965, marked the end of that type.

A further 43 Routemaster coaches followed down Park Royal's production line, the first being delivered the same month. These were 30ft-long vehicles, which enabled the seating capacity to be increased by an extra row on each deck to 65, with 36 upstairs and 29 below. They were classified RCL, the numbers continuing as RCL2218-2260. The general specification was similar to that of the RMC version in most

respects concerning comfort and finish, with power-operated entrance doors and hence an emergency door in the rear panel of the lower deck. They were the heaviest front-engined Routemasters, at 8 tons unladen, a modest figure for a double-decker though that nowadays seems, and were given the 11.3-litre AV690 engine rated at 150bhp at the usual 1,800rpm in consequence. As with the RMCs, they had rear air suspension and the higher-geared 4.7 to 1 rear axle.

When the last RCL was completed in June 1965, production switched to the RML 30ft bus version, 500 of which were to comprise London Transport's final bulk order for Routemaster buses. These were in all main respects similar to the previous RML880-903 batch, though updated in such minor respects as the later 'AEC-style' grille (adopted from 1963 for general

Facing page, top:
In 1964, RMF1254 was used for tests with a luggage-carrying trailer as part of a programme of experiments to arrive at the most practical form of vehicle to deal with the growing traffic in passengers between British European Airways' terminal at Gloucester Road and London Airport, Heathrow. It was considered too long for this role and the resulting BEA Routemasters were of the shorter 27ft 6½in length. *Ian Allan Library*

Left:
The choice of a Routemaster variant for the British European Airways coach fleet came as no surprise, as it was under London Transport management in regard to vehicle policy. The first of the type, KGJ 601D, is seen at BEA's Gloucester Road terminal when new in 1966, in company with AEC Regal IV coaches of the type the new vehicles replaced. *W. H. R. Godwin*

production) from RM1680 and in fact the later grille was subsequently fitted to earlier buses too in a rare exercise in updating. On early production RMs, cooling grilles intended to improve the air flow to the front brakes were provided in the area just below the headlamps but these were later found unnecessary and were deleted. The removal of the indentation where they had been was a logical consequence, but in the event provided another variation.

Of more consequence was the provision of illuminated advertisement panels on the offside of RM1577 in 1963, followed by 199 more such vehicles in 1964, and as the fluorescent lighting implied modified electrical equipment these rated a new code, 9RM9, the original vehicles involved being RM1923-2121. A further 100 similar panels were incorporated in RML2561-2660 in 1966-67, though these bodies were distinguished only by a 'stroke' variation. The idea was not the success hoped for, this also being found by other operators, and generally fell into disuse, though a more modest scheme for internal illuminated advertisements worked better and became a typical Routemaster feature.

RML production had not long been underway in 1965, progressing only from the first of the 500, RML2261, to RML2305, producing 45 red vehicles, before a switch was made to green for the first batch of production country area Routemaster buses. When RT production was coming to an end back in 1954, London Transport's needs for new vehicles were already dropping and there had been 81 green RT buses newly built that were placed in store; many of these had not

Far left:
What was then a small
concern in Perth,
Stagecoach Ltd, made its
first purchase of
Routemasters in January
1985, thereby introducing
the type to Scotland, soon to
become a major market for
ex-London Routemasters,
while Stagecoach was to
become one of the major
company groups under
deregulation. Among the
first areas to be the scene of
competitive services was
Glasgow, and Stagecoach
Routemaster 274 CLT,
formerly RM1274, is seen in
Glasgow city centre in
September 1988. The
fleetname Magicbus was
applied to the company's
services in the area.
T. K. & A. D. Brookes

Left:
Another Routemaster
acquisition made by
Stagecoach was the
ex-Northern General
Transport vehicle, RCN 699,
that had been operated for a
time by Stevenson of
Uttoxeter. It is also seen in
Glasgow in September
1988. *T. K. & A. D. Brookes*

entered service until 1958-59. It had therefore seemed logical to omit the country area from the early stages of the Routemaster programme, but now it was time to catch up. There were two batches of 50 green RML buses, numbered RML2306-2355 and RML2411-2460, and all entered service in the winter of 1965-66. They were basically similar to the central area version except that they had the semi-automatic version of the Monocontrol gearbox, leaving the driver to make his own decisions on the appropriate choice of ratio to use. It was considered that this was preferable in view of the more varied terrain in the country area, where driving in heavy traffic was less frequent and the benefit of the fully-automatic system less marked. The appearance on the scene of these buses had quite a marked effect on the country area bus fleet, for apart from the formerly stored buses, which of course were not truly new, the green RML batches were the first new double-deckers for that fleet for over 10 years and the first new type to enter service in quantity since 1950.

Output of RML models for central area service resumed, and both RML2356-2410 and RML2461 upwards were all red buses. Delivery continued steadily until RML2598 had been completed but was then interrupted while the final 'outside' order for Routemasters went through. In fact, this was virtually another London Transport order, in the sense that the specification was almost purely of Chiswick origin. British European Airways had a fleet of coaches to take passengers to or from London Airport at Heathrow, these vehicles starting or finishing their journeys at the terminal building at Gloucester Road. A fleet of 65 one-and-a-half-deck coaches on AEC Regal IV underfloor-engined chassis had been bodied by Park Royal to an LTE specification in 1952-53. Larger aircraft and growing traffic were calling for more seating capacity than the 37 seats in these vehicles, and it was decided to use double-deckers.

An AEC Regent V with Park Royal forward-entrance body having a luggage compartment built into the rear of the lower deck had been produced in 1961 as a possible prototype, but this rather austere vehicle was to remain unique. Tests were carried out in 1964 with RMF1254, towing a luggage trailer, the latter being a feature sometimes found in other countries but hitherto illegal in Britain – in fact the law was changed largely with the BEA project in mind. It was decided that the concept was close to what was wanted but that the overall length was too great in view of the added length of the trailer. So it was decided to revert to the shorter 27ft 6½in length of the standard RM, but with forward entrance layout. The modular concept of the Routemaster structure meant that the result was a cross between RMF1254 and a short RM in essentials, but with interiors and some other features very similar to the Green Line versions.

The order was for 65 vehicles, the same number as the Regal IV models which were to be replaced, so the increase of seating capacity to 56 gave an indication of the increasing popularity of air travel, even though but a fraction of what was to follow later. The seating was arranged with 32 up and 24 down, using seats of Green Line style but with grey and red moquette. There were luggage racks for small items but the bulk of luggage was carried in a two-wheeled trailer built by Marshall. The M4 motorway had created the possibility of much faster journeys to and from Heathrow and the BEA Routemasters were of modified specification to take advantage of that. The engines were of the AV690 11.3-litre type and were set to give 175bhp at a governed speed of 2,200rpm instead of the familiar 1,800rpm applying to other AEC double-deckers.

In addition the rear axle ratio of 4.08 to 1 instead of the standard RM's 5.22 to 1 further increased the speed potential – in fact the combination of governed speed and gearing implied an increase of top speed from the typical RM's 45mph or so to a nominal 69mph. In practice, the increase in power meant that even with the higher gearing, acceleration was quite brisk and the BEA vehicles held their own well in motorway traffic flows, even when fully laden. It is worthy of note that this 175bhp power output was not only the greatest of any Routemaster variant, but was also higher than on any production AEC double-decker. Even when the Regent V model was offered with AV691 engine, of similar size to the AV690, from 1966, it was derated to 128bhp at 1,800rpm, barely more than the standard full output of the immediate postwar Regent III when announced 20 years earlier.

Other features of the BEA vehicles included air suspension and the four-headlight feature of the Green Line version. More unusual, not only among the RM family but still rare on any British home-market bus or coach at that date was a combustion heater to augment the conventional system supplied by the engine coolant – no doubt the aim was to allow for situations where the vehicles might be waiting for lengthy periods for passengers delayed in the air by bad weather. No destination display was provided, unlike the Regal IV models which preceded them, which originally had carried the name of the flight destination, giving quite an exotic air as they ran through the outskirts of London bearing such names as 'Athens' or 'Lisbon', but by the 1960s travel on these vehicles was little different to that of any other bus, the link to specific flights having gone. Oddly, the obvious opportunity to carry an illuminated BEA name panel at the front was not taken, the logo being simply painted in this position, though at first illuminated displays were incorporated in the upper-deck side panels.

When originally delivered between October 1966 and April 1967, they were in quite an attractive mid-blue and white livery with black band against which the red BEA emblem stood out quite well. In 1969, BEA adopted a new corporate image using much bolder lettering and a similar mainly red livery, using a poppy red shade very close to that adopted two years later by the National Bus Company although retaining white above the upper deck waist-rail. Slightly larger trailers, by Locomotors, replaced the originals in 1972 and then in 1973-74 as the merger

of BEA with Bristol Overseas Airways produced the new British Airways, the livery changed back to blue, this time using a darker shade, and more white, this time down to the lower deck waist level. In typical AEC style, the chassis numbers allocated for this final production Routemaster order were the highest of the series, though having the new R2RH/2 prefix applicable to the BEA variant – they were thus R2RH/2/2807-2871.

After the last BEA version went through, Park Royal reverted to output of RML buses, continuing from RML2599 to the final vehicle, RML2760. The rate of entry into service slowed somewhat and it was not until May 1968 that the last entered service, though delivery of the last four had been completed in January of that year. London Transport had switched its main attention to rear-engined buses, in line with national trends, and although the intention of putting much greater emphasis on single-deckers had already begun to be toned down from the rather extreme line taken in 1965-66, the RML was already apt to be regarded as old-fashioned, because of its half-cab rear-entrance layout, before the last few entered service.

Above and left:
The interior design of the Routemaster changed little during its production run. These views show RML2692, one of the final batch and convey the typical upper-deck view seen by a passenger moving to his or her seat and the lower deck as seen by someone about to get off. The quarter-drop opening windows were designed to avoid the obstruction to vision at seated passengers' eye level which had been a drawback of the half-drop used on earlier London buses. The lower deck view shows the longitudinal seats for four passengers found on the RML version. *Park Royal*

Right:
When RM652 was borrowed in 1985, at first simply in connection with an open day, by the newly-formed Clydeside Scottish, it was not realised what impact it was to have on the whole bus scene in Scotland. Trials on the company's routes led to orders for similar buses for this and two other Scottish Bus Group companies totalling 137 vehicles. RM652 is shown in Clydeside livery but retaining its original fleet number in a manner quite common with the type.
G. Rixon

Below right:
Kelvin Scottish, another of the SBG companies favouring ex-London RMs, adopted a more radical livery style. The former RM357 is seen leaving Glasgow for Bridgeton.
G. Rixon

Far right:
Meanwhile, operation of Routemasters in London continued, with the RML-type buses having a more assured future than the shorter standard RM. Here, RML2647 has its radiator topped up before going into service from Upton Park garage in April 1988. In addition to a destination display in yellow lettering it carries advertising publicity drawing attention to the 15 route as a tourist facility.
K. Lane

CHAPTER FOUR

THE ROUTEMASTERS THAT MIGHT HAVE BEEN

It was inevitable that ideas on bus design had moved on somewhat in the interval between the original planning of the Routemaster in the early 1950s and the delayed period of production. The rear-engined layout had been tried in various prototypes built by Midland Red and in an experimental Leyland in the 1930s, whilst London Transport's interest in the idea got as far as the remarkable batch of CR-class rear-engined Leyland Cub 20-seat buses in 1939. After the war, Foden introduced a rear-engined coach design which might have attracted more attention had it not been associated with that concern's two-stroke diesel engine — the whole package was simply a bit too 'far out' for even the more adventurous coach proprietor, apart from a very few brave exceptions. It was available with Gardner engine, but even this was not what operators wanted, and the contemporary interest in the mid-underfloor engine position on the part of major operators took the spotlight off any move to put the engine farther to the rear.

Abroad, however, opinions were different. In the United States, the rear engine had been widely accepted from the mid-1930s, with General Motors' adoption of the idea and its acceptance by no less an organisation than the Greyhound Corporation as well as city transport fleets from New York downwards making anything else seem outdated by 1939 or so. In Europe, there had been more interest in the mid-underfloor engine, but there was greater readiness to depart from the front engine, partly because the double-decker was generally out of favour. It was significant that Leyland's renewed interest in the rear-engined layout for experimental double-deckers was due to the appointment of an eminent German

engineer, Dr Ing A. Mueller, as Chief Development & Research Engineer to Leyland Motors Ltd in 1953 — he had been working for them since 1947.

The early PDR1 prototypes visited quite a large number of operators in the period around 1953-55 and aroused interest, but could not be said to have excited the industry. The 1956 version, taking advantage of the extra length newly permitted and adopting the more radical idea of combining the rear engine position with an entrance ahead of the front axle, aroused much more interest, not least because of the idea of accommodating seats for 78 passengers — at least half a dozen more than could be fitted into a front-engined bus of 30ft length. The 1958 Commercial Motor Show brought the production version of the Leyland Atlantean and immediate success in terms of volume of orders, even though it was far from being a thoroughly developed design, as early users were to find out.

Then, in 1960, Daimler introduced the Fleetline, of very similar general layout but with Gardner 6LX engine, having an already excellent reputation, and a drop-centre rear axle giving the capability of being a low-floor model where desired. Taken together, the Atlantean and Fleetline had a profound effect on the double-deck bus market and AEC was far from being in a strong position.

As mentioned in Chapter 3, the AEC venture into low-floor double-deckers had not been encouraging. In any case, the market for such vehicles was not as large as manufacturers were apt to think. There seem to be grounds for thinking that both AEC and, to a lesser extent, Leyland were misled by the success of the Bristol Lodekka, the first of the generation of

24 Camden Town
Charing Cross Road
Whitehall Victoria

CHALK FARM GARAGE

CUV 12 C

Left:
The Leyland Atlantean set
the British city bus
operators on a path of
recognising the advantages
of the rear-engined double-
decker. Yet the original
PDR1/1 production model
was far from reliable even
after six years of
manufacture; London
Transport was to suffer
considerable trouble when
50 were placed in service.
Here XA12 is seen in Victoria
Street in November 1965,
during the comparative
trials when XA and RML
buses were operated
successively on Routes 24
and 76. *P. J. Relf*

front-engined low-floor models, of which the prototype had appeared in 1950 and which became the Tilling Group's standard double-decker from 1954. Tilling had standardised on lowbridge double-deckers, generally speaking, since the mid-1930s, in some cases because of need but partly because its management set great store on standardisation as a

principle and the idea of a model that could be common to almost all fleets within the group appealed in itself. The BET group had never been like that, partly because it gave greater freedom to individual company managements to decide their own vehicle policy, within limits, and partly because there had been no significant need for low-height double-deckers in

Right:
The repainting of
Routemasters in the original
style for publicity purposes
was becoming recognised as
an effective way of
attracting attention to
special services. Here
RM254 is seen looking very
largely 'as new' when
operating on a Kingston
shoppers' express service in
April 1984. *G. Rixon*

Far right:
The conversion of
Routemasters to open-
topped form doubtless set
engineers checking stress
calculations at Chiswick in
view of the integral
construction. It was
probably more than
consideration for windswept
passengers that led to the
retention of the side window
framing over the first two
bays of the upper deck,
though this also gave rather
a stylish effect with the use
of a curved outline like that
normally used for the
rearmost bay for the second
window. RM1864 is seen in
this form in Regent Street in
August 1988. *G. Rixon*

Facing page
The rear-engined Routemaster was doomed as a project even before the only example to be completed was revealed to the public. Even so, its importance as a pointer to the future led the author to request facilities to carry out a road test for *Bus & Coach,* **the monthly journal he then edited. FRM1 is seen just after climbing the 1 in 6 gradient at the Motor Industry Research Association's proving ground at Lindley, near Nuneaton on 1 June 1967.**

many of its areas, quite often previously served by trams which had needed more headroom than even the tallest standard needed for buses. There were municipalities which needed low-height buses but they were in a minority and relatively small in relation to the big city fleets.

The Bridgemaster had not been sold in large numbers and yet what amounted to a second-guess exercise had been put in hand, culminating in the introduction of the Renown low-floor chassis in 1962. This stepped back from the idea of advancing technology to the extent not only of having a separate chassis, understandable in regard to operators' commitment to local bodybuilders and in some cases a wish for something less austere than the Bridgemaster's standard production finish, but also in relation to front suspension. A beam front axle with leaf springs gave quite a hard ride at the front, and the noise level for both driver and passengers (except those seated near the rear) was much higher than that experienced in one of the 'new generation' Atlanteans or Fleetlines. It was hardly surprising that the Renown did not do well in comparative trials and sales were much the same as for the Bridgemaster. It is ironical that, setting the Routemaster and the 'special relationship' between AEC and LTE aside, it was the Regent, still in many respects basically the same general design as had been introduced as the Mk III range in 1946-47, that was continuing to be the mainstay of AEC sales in the double-deck market.

Part of the trouble was a lack of enthusiasm for double-deckers among the AEC management, and in fairness it must be said that there was a rather vocal school of thought in the operating industry which thought that the British love affair with the double-deck bus was an anachronism. When the 30ft single-decker first became legal with two-axle layout in 1950, there had been those who thought that the 'standee' single-decker would render the double-decker obsolete. The travelling public made its dislike of the demonstration vehicles of this type quite clear, and in any case it was found that such buses could not show any saving in running costs.

The idea was revived with the advent of the 36ft (11m) single-decker in 1961-62, following a further relaxation in the length limit. This time there was not only the greater size of the vehicle now permissible but an important new factor had appeared. The idea of operating a bus without a conductor was of growing appeal as a way of cutting costs and, indeed, of

helping to overcome staff shortages which often tended to be a problem. Until the 1950s, it had only been permissible to operate vehicles with up to 26 seats without a conductor, but this had been extended to single-deckers in general. In practice, their use generally depended on trade union agreements and although the unions had been doing all they could to gain bonus payments for drivers there was general acceptance that vehicles with up to 45 seats could be one-man-operated.

Clearly, if a 36ft single-decker could run with a driver only, there would be useful cost savings as compared to a double-decker with a crew of two. This proposition aroused fresh interest and for a time in the early and mid-1960s, there was quite a strong school of thought that the double-decker might be on the way out. On the other hand, there were probably more who were unconvinced but on the whole this was something of a silent majority. Opinions were often quite divided within both operating and manufacturing organisations. Not surprisingly, managements tried to cover themselves by backing both lines of thought to some degree.

Thus, though London Transport's management was seriously examining the idea of much greater use of single-deckers by 1963-64, it was agreed that the development of a rear-engined version of the Routemaster was worth pursuing. Similarly, at ACV, the parent company of both AEC and Park Royal, it was agreed that this project had possibilities in terms of sales to those operators who saw the rear-engined double-decker as having a better prospect of being the city bus of the future. Generally, at that stage, most people in the industry were still thinking in terms of such a vehicle requiring a conductor, and indeed, this was still a legal requirement until 1966. However, there had been some speculation as to whether it might be possible to overcome the objections to the idea, one of which was the question of adequate supervision of the upper deck, perhaps by running such a bus with driver only in the off-peak period by closing the stairs by some form of door or gate. The more radical idea of simply running the bus full-time on a one-person basis had been put forward but was still being regarded with scepticism, not so much as to its feasibility but as to whether either officialdom or, almost as significant in those days, the trade unions would accept the idea. It should not be forgotten that quite a few important operators had encountered considerable difficulty in getting union acceptance for the use of rear-engined double-deckers seating over 70 passengers with a crew of two in the 1959-61 period.

With this background, the seemingly cautious approach to the idea of a rear-engined Routemaster was understandable. It is also worth mentioning that there had been an earlier possibility of AEC being involved in the development of an advanced-design double-decker, for when the West Riding Automobile Co Ltd, in those days a major independent operator which had been a keen user of AEC Regent III models, began thinking about its special needs in the late 1950s, an approach had been made to AEC. Understandably this was not taken up and West Riding turned to Guy, the Wulfrunian being the result of the close co-operation that followed. This model, with its engine on the front platform, air suspension and disc brakes, proved a bit too unorthodox to be successful, at any rate in the circumstances of its birth. It is interesting to speculate on whether a larger manufacturer could have poured enough money and expertise into the project to make it a reliable and economic vehicle.

The rear-engined Routemaster began with a number of important advantages. The standard Routemaster's modular construction and advanced specification meant that both could form much of the basis of the new version. By 1964, when detailed work on the design and construction of what were originally to be three prototypes was started, the Routemaster was a well-proven design, and in addition to the standard version, there was experience of the variants to draw upon. Quite a high proportion of components already in production were incorporated, and attention concentrated on the parts of the design which were new.

The wheelbase was 16ft 10in, the same as a standard RM, and, in effect, the rear-engined version was produced by grafting on a new front end and accommodating the engine in the space normally occupied by the rear platform. That is an over-simplification, of course, but it proved possible to avoid the short bay used in the RML design and thus the FRM, as it was eventually designated, was built up from standard-length bays giving an overall length of 31ft 3in. In this respect, the designers' task was simplified as compared to that facing the designers of such models as the Leyland Atlantean, which had to comply strictly with the 30ft length limit then in force. The relaxation of this restriction to 11m, or 36ft 1in, had yet to be

Right:
The RCL-class former Green Line coaches made almost ideal sightseeing vehicles. RCL2248 negotiates the buses-only lane at Hyde Park Corner. *G. Rixon*

Far right:
The RMA class, with staircase in place, and consequently having the characteristic blank panel behind the cab, was another 'natural' for sightseeing work. RMA15 is seen at Victoria. *A. L. Such*

fully exploited in a British double-decker, but it made it possible to choose a figure which suited the 'natural' result of an assembly of components already in existence.

Even so, the changes in configuration meant that quite a number of fundamental alterations had to be made. The 'wheelbarrow' front sub-frame assembly carrying the engine and steering of the RM was no longer a logical concept, and for the FRM a full-length underframe was designed which took the front and rear suspension loadings as well as those of other units more directly. The front suspension was much the same as a standard RM, with coil-spring independent wishbone assemblies in each side. At the rear, the pivoted sub-frame principle was retained, but air suspension similar to that on the coach versions of the front-engined Routemaster was used.

The basic idea of using a transversely-mounted vertical engine was much the same as on the Atlantean or Fleetline, with the engine, in this case an AEC AV691 unit, mounted towards the nearside of the vehicle, with the gearbox in the offside corner. These models differed in the design of the layout of the drive from the engine through the gearbox to the rear axle. Space and the need for access for maintenance or removal of defective units makes the design of a rear-engined bus far from easy. The AEC solution was simpler than others

and yet gave good access. The engine was mounted slightly higher than usual, and with the gearbox at a normal lower level, this allowed the use of a propeller shaft from the fluid flywheel taking the drive from the engine, over the main casing of the gearbox, to a train of gears on its right-hand (off-side) face. The drive was thus taken through the gearbox in a conventional way, emerging via a pair of spiral bevel gears to the second, main, propeller shaft leading forward to the rear axle. This was basically a standard Routemaster unit turned round to that the drive entered from the rear rather than the front.

Inevitably, this longer and more complex vehicle, with such features as quite a complicated heating and ventilating system and power-operated doors, was bound to be heavier than a front-engined Routemaster. The prototype weighed 8ton 10cwt, compared to 7ton 15cwt for the RML, but a fairer comparison was perhaps that with the RCL 30ft Green Line version at 8 tons. London Transport engineers reckoned that in production, it might have been possible to trim another 3cwt or so off the total unladen weight, bringing it to around 8ton 7cwt. Even as it stood, 8½ tons was a very modest figure for a soundly designed and exceptionally well-finished rear-engined double-decker. Contemporary Atlantean and Fleetline designs were at least as heavy, even when finish was much more austere, and some examples were creeping up to the 9-ton mark. It is significant that London Transport's production DMS-class Daimler Fleetline double-deckers weighed between 9ton 11cwt and 9ton 15cwt and that Leyland National single-deckers weighed more than the Routemaster — even the short 10.3m version as used by LT turned the scales at 8ton 13cwt.

To give the livelier performance by then being favoured, the AV691 engine, the dry-cylinder liner successor to the AV690 unit and of the same 11.3-litre capacity was used, set to give the same 150bhp output at 1,800rpm as the AV690 had given in the RCL 30ft Green Line Routemasters. The drive train was otherwise in line with normal RM-series bus standards in having the combination of fluid flywheel and fully automatic four-speed epicyclic gearbox with the usual system of electro-pneumatic control, retaining the characteristic LT style of selector lever with its echo of the RT preselector lever. The rear axle ratio was the standard Routemaster 5.22 to 1, giving a maximum speed of 46mph.

Other aspects of the driver's controls, and indeed the general mechanical specification, were also of RM-series style. London Transport engineers continued to be convinced that the all-hydraulic brake system was better than any alternative and was incorporated, the continuous-flow hydraulic pump being mounted on top of the gearbox in this application. Interestingly, the handbrake continued to be a simple unassisted mechanical unit, but the traditional-style lever was capable of holding on a gradient of 1 in 5, steeper than the laden bus could climb. The power-assisted steering was also basically as on a standard RM.

Apart from being laid out differently, the major innovations of the FRM concerned the engine cooling system and the heating and ventilating arrangements. As usual, the two were inter-related, and it doubtless seemed logical to take a radical approach once the engine and hence the 'obvious' position for the radiator were removed from the front of the vehicle. The Clayton Dewandre concern was developing its Compas system — the name was simply an abbreviation of 'comfort for passengers' — and as this replaced the conventional radiator with two heat exchangers designed to be mounted remotely from the engine, it had obvious attraction for a rear-engined vehicle.

The two heat exchangers, each with a hydraulically driven fan, were mounted at the rear of the upper deck, under the five-passenger rear seat. Ducting fed air, heated if desired, to the upper and lower decks and this drew air in under the louvre which ran above the lower-deck windows. Rather optimistically, opening windows were eliminated, and with hindsight it seems clear that the scene was set for a repeat of the RTC1 episode of 1949. However, there was quite widespread optimism that the development of technology as it stood in the mid-1960s would enable that which had proved unacceptably troublesome to be achieved. In fact, overheating and the production of reliable heating systems was to prove one of the main areas of weakness of British rear-engined buses, and especially double-deckers right up to the mid-1970s. Suffice it to say at this stage that the FRM did not prove immune.

Although relatively orthodox in layout, taking existing rear-engined double-deckers as the norm, much careful thought was devoted to the interior design of the FRM. The floor level could be described as of medium height, originally derived simply from the standard RM, but it had been found that this reduced the problems of footstool and wheelarch intrusion that arose when an ultra-low floor was attempted. London Transport had always paid careful attention to step and doorway layout as well as the flow of movement up the stairs.

Good visibility for the driver was another aim, and the barrel-shaped windscreen was to be a prototype for succeeding generations of London bus designs. At the opposite end of the bus, some ingenuity was devoted to cutting back the heavy-looking corner pillars that were apt to be produced if a smooth rear profile was attempted on a rear-engined bus on the Atlantean/Fleetline model, despite the way in which the

Right:

A little further to the west, an independent operator, Verwood Transport carried out a modification to a former British Airways Routemaster that seemed an obvious step for use on normal bus duties yet was never carried out on the RMA vehicles used in London on such duties. The former RMA58 shows off its front destination screen as well as an attractive livery when seen in Bournemouth. *R. Hefford*

Far right:

As Stagecoach acquired former NBC subsidiary companies, it tended to spread its favour for the Routemaster to more parts of England that had never seen such buses in service previously. In Carlisle, the former RM1983 is seen in English Street in December 1987, having become 903 in the Cumberland Motor Services fleet, locally-based vehicles having the CMS Carlislebus fleetname. *R. J. Waterhouse*

rear window was deeply recessed. The seating layout was not aimed at the maximum possible capacity, partly in the interest of freedom of circulation, though doubtless the prospect of trade union difficulties also discouraged anything too adventurous in London Transport service at that date. So the total of 72 seats was just the same as that of the RML, though the split between the decks was slightly different, with one fewer on the lower deck at 31, and one more upstairs with 41.

Construction of three prototypes was authorised and put in hand in 1964, as mentioned, a fact which is itself of significance and perhaps rather surprising in view of subsequent events. The takeover of the AEC empire by Leyland had taken place in July 1962. Clearly, future model policy was a matter for the management of the Leyland Motor Corporation which was set up following the merger, and indeed joint action was quite rapid in the case of the 1964 introduction of the Leyland Panther and AEC Swift and Merlin rear-engined single-deck models which used a common frame and other items though retaining engines of the respective makes. However, London Transport was yet to formulate its major change of policy and, indeed, there were clear indications of some division of opinion within both the Leyland and LT empires.

So construction, at any rate of one vehicle, went ahead. Park Royal allocated three body numbers, B53296-98, in advance of building in its usual way, it being noteworthy that these were in the 'general' B series rather than the L series which had begun with the RT contracts just after World War 2, reaching L3280 (which was on RTL1600, delivered in September 1954) by the end of the RT series and continuing with RM8 (which had Park Royal body number L3281) in 1958. The front-engined Routemasters built for London Transport were all numbered in the L series, the final number being L6038 which was RML2760 delivered in January 1968, but the examples built for Northern General and British European Airways were B-numbered vehicles.

Although no public announcement was made, it became known that a rear-engined Routemaster was to appear at the Commercial Motor Show to be held in September 1966, and it was to be in Sheffield Corporation livery. Meanwhile construction of the vehicle for London Transport went ahead, its original classification being RMR (Routemaster rear-engined) but this changed to the FRM (Front-entrance Routemaster) actually used before completion. This was Park

Royal B53296, becoming FRM1 and being registered KGY 4D. It was delivered without any publicity to Chiswick in June 1966, having been given the type code 10RM11 and was given the London Transport body number A88, following a series of experimental vehicles beginning with a batch of 50 Leyland Atlanteans and including the first AEC Merlin single-deckers.

Herein lay the clue to the threat to further progress, for London Transport was about to issue its Bus Reshaping Plan, which called for extensive use of single-deckers and consequently a much reduced role for the double-decker. The decisions on this change of direction had been taken before FRM1 had been delivered and although there was to be a certain amount of back-tracking after the Plan was published in September, it was clear that double-deckers were to be put on the back burner for a while so far as London Transport was concerned. This gave Sir Donald Stokes, who had emerged from a successful career as Leyland's bus sales chief to become Chairman of the Leyland Motor Corporation, sufficient grounds to scrap the whole project. It is perhaps over-simplistic to say that there was an anti-AEC feeling at Leyland, but the judgement was made that the Leyland Atlantean was to continue as the group's main challenger in the double-deck business, and of course the change of view from London put the whole industry's ideas in doubt.

With hindsight, it is easy to conclude that this was a short-sighted decision. Yet even if one tries to recall the atmosphere of the time, it does seem unfortunate that the project was not kept going. It is particularly ironic that legislation permitting the use of double-deckers on a driver-only basis came into effect on 1 July 1966, cutting the ground from under the feet of the pro-single-deck school of thought at almost the very peak of its influence. Oddly enough, London Transport had itself played a part in this, with its plan to run eight experimental Daimler Fleetline double-deckers in the country area on a part-time one-man basis, the specification of the Park Royal bodywork for them providing for this when the order was placed in 1964-65. It would not have been legal to do so, even with the top deck closed off as originally planned, at that time, but revised regulations were published in November 1965 and hence it was clear that it was to become possible to operate such buses and, more important, suitably designed double-deckers generally, in this way.

Orders already in the pipeline naturally had a delaying

effect on the ensuing change of direction and at the 1966 Show (from which the rear-engined Routemaster had been withdrawn) there was still talk of some other operators of city buses perhaps switching to single-deckers entirely. But soon moves were afoot to exploit the new possibilities and, in particular, Manchester Corporation announced that same autumn that 96 double-deckers then on order were to be operated on a one-man basis. The general manager of that undertaking was Mr R. F. Bennett and he was to bring his enthusiasm for the double-decker with him when appointed to the board of London Transport in September 1968. There had already been some indication of modification of the Bus Reshaping Plan, toning down the switch to single-deckers, but Bennett's influence was soon evident in the initial order for what was to become the DMS class of Daimler Fleetline double-deckers, due for delivery in 1969, though in practice the first vehicles did not arrive until 1970.

Thus the whole picture had changed again and one wonders whether the decision not to proceed with the rear-engined Routemaster would have been made, had it cropped up say even a year later. Just how much of a market the model might have had outside any London business is a matter for speculation, but AEC had quite a number of loyal customers among city fleet operators and if Sheffield was interested enough to give the model a try, it is not difficult to imagine that say Glasgow, Leeds and Nottingham would have been among potential customers. Northern General was very enthusiastic about its front-engined Routemasters and there were several other BET companies which might have been interested, particularly in the light of a far from trouble-free history from many of the users of early Atlanteans — the London Transport batch were soon to become quite notorious for breakdowns in service, and the author was told that serious consideration was given to selling them after only a couple of years or so. It was considered that this would have been difficult to justify without spelling out the true reason with consequent embarrassment all round, since at that time they and the small batch of Fleetlines were LT's only 'modern' double-deckers other than FRM1 itself, of course.

So the sole FRM was condemned to be almost a museum piece from new. It was shown to the technical press in December 1966, and work on it continued at first as a Chiswick-based experimental vehicle until it entered service from Tottenham garage mainly on Route 76 alongside the Atlanteans in June 1967. Sadly, it cannot be said that it was trouble-free. Quite apart from the inadequacy of ventilation which soon became evident, the all too common bugbear of overheating common to almost all early rear-engined bus designs was experienced. A fire in the engine compartment was experienced on 31 August and the bus was taken out of service for repair and modification. When it reappeared from Chiswick, opening windows of standard Routemaster type had been fitted.

When LT decided to adopt one-man operation of double-deckers, FRM1 was converted to suit this and joined some Atlanteans which had also been converted for an early pilot route, running from Croydon garage from December 1969. It then ran from there until 1973, when it was out of service for a time before reappearing after overhaul and transferring to Potters Bar garage, where it ran until September 1976, when collision damage again put it out of service for a time. It then was equipped with a stereo cassette player for use on the Round London Sightseeing Tour but increasingly tended to be treated as a historic vehicle, as indeed it is.

Whether the model would have been successful, had it gone into production in 1967 or even, say, after a pause in 1969-70 is a matter for speculation. Teething troubles there would doubtless have been, but perseverance could have overcome them, just as the Atlantean was turned into an outstandingly successful vehicle in AN68 form from 1972. In terms of specification, the model would still be well up to current standards in the 1990s and the cost of manufacture, which may have seemed high in the context of 1966, would have benefited from the use of many common parts from the standard Routemaster. Looked at in hindsight, and by comparison with the B15/Titan project which was developed by Leyland to meet a London-based requirement which amounted to the FRM reborn, but which had nothing in manufacturing terms in common, it would have been positively cheap.

It is ironic that the design process that eventually led to the development of the rear-engined Leyland Titan had begun with a Park Royal project early in the 1970s to produce an updated FRM, which could have been produced quite quickly. However Leyland decided instead to embark on a completely new design, the B15, which did not go into production as the Titan until 1978.

Far left:
Stagecoach subsidiaries in England at first retained local liveries which had been introduced shortly before privatisation and retaining a vestige of the traditional local colour. Thus United Counties buses were still basically green when Routemasters were introduced under Stagecoach ownership at Corby. The former RM1685 is seen on the first day of RM operation in Corby, 11 April 1988. *T. Carter*

Left:
East Yorkshire Motor Services Ltd had a distinctive dark blue and cream livery that had been swept away in the 'corporate image' era of the NBC. The decision to take eight Routemasters as a means of dealing with competitive circumstances in the Hull area was linked to revival of the traditional colours, albeit without the white roof used in former times. The result was surprisingly effective, even though the Routemaster body had never been designed for the 'three cream bands' style of livery application. The one-time RM982 is seen as EYMS 804 at Longhill in May 1988.
R. J. Waterhouse

CHAPTER FIVE

ROUTEMASTER RETROSPECT

Facing page, top:
The controls of a typical Routemaster, as seen by the driver as he climbs into his seat. The gear selector lever position was much the same as inherited from the RT, though the actual unit mounted under the left of the steering wheel was of different shape and was normally intended for relatively infrequent use, the driver selecting automatic at the beginning of the journey (though it had been converted to semi-automatic operation on this particular vehicle, RM850, at the time of the photograph). Note the traditional-style handbrake on the left. On the right, a tachograph had replaced the original speedometer – no other instruments were provided. *Stephen Morris*

It is not unusual for the last examples of a vehicle type to enter service after the model in question has become obsolete, but the change in London bus policy that was in progress in 1968 as the last RML-type Routemasters took the road was profound. London Transport had embarked on the Bus Reshaping Programme and the first production deliveries of the AEC rear-engined single-deckers had begun to arrive in February 1968. The original idea of replacement of the majority of LT's double-deckers with single-deckers was already being watered down, but the inevitable time lag between changes of policy and their implementation meant that single-deckers were to be predominant among deliveries until the early 1970s.

The swing back to double-deckers had begun rather cautiously at first, no doubt influenced by the unsatisfactory experience with the Leyland Atlanteans. It seems to have been taken for granted that the rear-engined layout was essential for driver-only operation of any type of city bus, and an initial order for 17 Daimler Fleetlines had been placed for delivery in 1969, as a follow-up to the earlier experimental batch of nine for the country area. In the event, the Fleetline was chosen as the main London bus type for the early to mid-1970s, a line of policy reinforced by the arrival of Ralph Bennett, who had been a major pioneer of one-man double-deck operation while general manager with Manchester Corporation Transport Department, as a member of the London Transport Board from September 1968. Although the last Routemasters were then still virtually new, they were in some respects already an anachronism, or so it seemed. The rear-entrance double-decker, almost extinct as a production type, with only handfuls

of examples being built for various provincial operators, was effectively killed off completely for the British market by its exclusion from the New Bus Grant specifications issued in that year.

On the other hand, the Routemaster was proving a reliable and popular vehicle. London Transport had again paid the penalty for being a pioneer in brake system development, just as had happened with the air-brake system of the RT, for the all-hydraulic Routemaster system did require a fair amount of attention initially. Much work had been done in each case before the big volumes of production got under way – it was fortuitous that the delay in the need for Routemaster production due to the surplus of vehicles in the later 1950s had given several years of development time in just the same way as had the war years for the RT. Yet almost inevitably, some practical problems only came to light when vehicles entered normal service and it took a little while for maintenance staff to get the measure of them.

Within a little while, however, the Routemaster was proving directly comparable with the RT in terms of mileages run between breakdowns, and both types were vastly superior to any of the newer breeds of rear-engined models in service with London Transport up to 1970. The Daimler Fleetline started off quite well, but it, too, was soon to run into problems in London service. It can be argued that some of these difficulties were related to LT's failure to modify its maintenance methods to suit the more complex types of vehicle, yet the Routemaster had shown that a technically advanced design, in itself, was no barrier to obtaining good reliability even on the basis of little more than routine servicing at the garages and reliance on a central overhaul works for the rest.

Just how much the Routemaster's success was related to its design being tailor-made for London requirements was not easy to assess at that stage, with no comparison available with operation by concerns using differing methods and with different operating conditions. But when Northern General Transport (NGT) had gained a little experience with its 50 vehicles delivered in 1964-65, some interesting virtues came to light. Any observant passenger, let alone a driver, would soon be aware of the model's stability on a twisty route. This was and still is readily apparent in London, and the almost roll-free cornering capability is a benefit by no means always found in models of much later design.

London roads and streets were generally kept in quite good repair – perhaps better than in more recent times in some areas – and so the ability to soak up road undulations rarely was tested to any great degree. In NGT territory, however, the state of road repairs was apt to be adversely affected both by mining subsidence in some areas and also the effect of the harsher winters tending to break up the surface due to the effects of frost and heavier use of salt. The Routemasters coped well with this except that under some of the more undulating surfaces resulting from subsidence, some pitching became a little more evident, probably because of the basically softer ride.

As time went on, however, more specific benefits became apparent. The hydraulic brake system had been developed to a state of generally good reliability by the time the NGT buses were delivered, and this operator discovered a new benefit in its tougher climatic conditions. This was the freedom from the problem of frozen air systems which had been found to be a serious defect on vehicles with compressed-air brake operation. The hydraulic fluid will not freeze at any temperature foreseeable in Britain, so a source of nuisance and possibly even danger had been eliminated.

The heavy use of salt on the roads of County Durham to cope with the wintry conditions found in most winters in that part of the world generally had a very bad effect on steel-framed bodywork. At some 30 tons of salt for each mile of main road in the county during the course of a typical winter, a significant degree of salt could be found on the surface at any date between October and April. When rear-engined

Left:
The Chiswick preference for simple, robust switches is evident in this view. London bus drivers have been used to reaching upwards for the hook-shaped starter for well over half a century.
Stephen Morris

Right:
Southend Transport was another local authority-owned undertaking to turn to the Routemaster, adopting a brighter version of its traditional blue, coupled with a larger area of white (in place of cream) and adding a slim red band on the upper deck. Here number 108, the former RM1061, is seen in Southend bus station in company with two of this fleet's Northern Counties-bodied Fleetlines.
R. J. Waterhouse

Above centre:
One of the more intriguing of the purchases of Routemasters by provincial operators in the late 1980s has been that of Greater Manchester Buses. The red livery with single white band is more than merely exploitation of the undoubted public interest in the operation of London-type buses, for it is very close to the style favoured by Manchester Corporation when that body was responsible for the city's buses, a point underlined by the choice of red for the wheels. RM1618 is seen heading for West Didsbury in October 1988.
R. J. Waterhouse

Below centre:
Another form of provincial fascination with the 'London' image was the association of Eastenders for the Routemasters placed in service by Burnley & Pendle towards the end of 1988. A combination of traditional colours and the fashionable diagonal stripe is seen on 184, the former RM2114.
R. Hefford

Left:
Despite all the activity outside London in recent years, the Routemaster is still a familiar sight on the streets of the capital. Here RML901 shows how the 1988 version of London Buses livery retains almost all the traditional Routemaster look as it catches the October sunshine crossing Ludgate Circus. *K. Lane*

double-deckers, and particularly those of low-floor layout, came into use, a hitherto unknown series of events worsened the situation. The lack of engine heat at the front of the vehicle plus the absence of the tendency for at least a little oil leakage meant that salt-laden snow or road spray caused much more serious corrosion than experienced hitherto. Moreover, the low-level layout tended to create a condition where snow or slush was driven up into the floor frame structure. When early Leyland Atlantean models fell due for recertification (the issue of a fresh Certificate of Fitness needed to allow use as a Public Service Vehicle under the procedure then in force) after seven years' service, NGT was finding that corrosion repairs implied not only extensive replacement of the body floor framing but also often involved the pillars as far up as the waistline. This could bring the cost of preparation to £2,000, a modest-sounding sum by today's standards but the complete vehicle may well have cost no more than £6,000 or £7,000 when new, and inflation had not yet taken off in the way that applied later in the 1970s.

The NGT Routemasters proved to be a much better bet from the point of view of corrosion. The aluminium-alloy structure was far more resistant to attack and recertification overhaul costs were about £700. Whenever the author visited the company in his capacity as Editor of *Bus & Coach* during that period, the conversation with David Cox, chief engineer of NGT at the time, would sooner or later turn to the Routemasters and the general sentiment was 'I wish we had more of them'. Yet they had the limitations from the operational viewpoint of being unsuitable for driver-only operation; despite being of forward-entrance layout, the design did not lend itself to a satisfactory fare-collecting or ticket-issuing set-up. By the early 1970s, this was becoming an essential means of attacking the problem of ever-rising costs and many mechanically sound double-deckers of unsuitable layout went for scrap because of it.

It is a measure of NGT's regard for the Routemaster that one was subjected to a major rebuild to overcome this and allow one-man operation, as it was invariably called in those days. A similar conversion had been carried out using a Leyland Titan PD3, early in 1972, the resulting semi-forward control vehicle being called the Tynesider. Fortuitously, a Routemaster was involved in a fairly severe front-end collision while the PD3 conversion was in hand, and this was chosen as the basis for the second rebuild, christened the Wearsider. In this case, the driving position and staircase were moved rearwards in much the same way as had been done on the PD3, but the front end of the upper deck was not foreshortened as in that instance. Both vehicles used bonnet and front wing assemblies built up from Routemaster-style parts, the right-hand sections being produced as hand-moulded glass-fibre opposite-hand copies of the left-hand parts. The seating capacity remained the same, at 72 in total, but there were two extra seats upstairs at 43 in all, and 29 in the lower deck.

The vehicle in question happened to be the first of the batch, number 2085, and it re-entered service in rebuilt form in August 1972, surviving until 1978, when it was sold and scrapped. Others might have been converted, as orginally intended, but the cost was deemed to be too great, and they remained in service with NGT in original form, apart from livery changes and a renumbering until withdrawn in the normal way. This began in earnest in 1977, just a little over the 12-year life that had been both BET group and, later, NBC official practice. However, the last example did not leave NGT service until 1981 and 12 vehicles were purchased by London Transport and given fleet numbers RMF2761-2772 in 1979-80, although in the somewhat wasteful-seeming way so typical of LT around that period, they were never used in service and were sold off again.

Meanwhile, the Routemasters built for London service had

Facing page, bottom:
Perhaps the most startling Routemaster-based vehicle was Northern General's *Wearsider,* rebuilt from the first of that company's examples in an effort to make it suitable for driver-only operation in 1972. The front of the lower deck was converted to semi-forward control, with the driver seated in much the same relation to the stubby bonnet as on a Bedford OB. The *Wearsider,* as it was called, is seen here at Chester-le-Street in April 1977. *M. Fowler*

Left:
The NBC corporate image livery caused the NGT Routemasters to revert to an almost all-red livery, but this time in the lighter poppy shade, from 1972. Local individuality was kept alive by the 'Shop at Binns' advertisement so long traditional on many local operators' fleets. Number 2111 (FPT 581C) is seen in Worswick Street bus station, Newcastle in company with a Willowbrook-bodied Bristol VRT and Leyland National buses. *A. Pearson*

Right:
RML900, an exception to the general rule of not selling off RML-class buses because of their greater seating capacity, due to it having been damaged so badly that London Buses did not deem it worth repairing, found a good home with Clydeside Scottish. Clearly the challenge of repairing it was taken up with determination and the result, christened *Clydesider* in a manner reminiscent of the NGT rebuild of RCN 685, is seen at the North Weald rally in June 1988. *K. Lane*

emerged from the period in which they were regarded as anachronisms at an official level to earn a general if somewhat grudging respect. The Bus Reshaping Plan of 1966 had indicated that withdrawals of Routemasters would be under way by the mid-1970s because of their unsuitability for driver-only operation. In any case, the early production deliveries would by then have been in service for about 15 years, which was the officially accepted life-span for which they were designed, even if this had been shown to be capable of considerable extension in the case of the RT, also in theory a 15-year design. As late as 1972, this scenario was still sufficiently accepted for it to be agreed that only light overhauls be carried out on about 60 vehicles which were expected to have been withdrawn when the three-year Certificates of Fitness they were given expired.

As usual with major classes in London service, different programmes of overhaul were in hand simultaneously to cover vehicles of varying ages. The first series of overhauls came to an end in 1974, as the last RML-type buses were put through. Meanwhile, earlier buses had begun to go through their second overhauls in 1968 and the third overhaul programme began in 1974, following on from the ending of the first. By then, a combination of factors had begun to uplift the Routemaster from a near has-been in the management's eyes to being regarded as the continuing solid foundation of many of London's best-known bus routes. The rear-engined buses, both single- and double-deck, were proving troublesome to a degree not experienced on any major London bus type since the war years. Even though this was in part related to London Transport's inability to respond to the changing needs of new types of vehicle, the problems were real enough. In addition, not only had the Reshaping Plan been virtually rewritten, with the role of single-deckers reduced to something much nearer the traditional minor level in the provision of the capital's bus services, but one-man operation, as it was still generally called, was itself proving more of an area of contention than elsewhere in Britain.

The reasons for all this, and indeed London Transport's general position as an organisation at the centre of controversy, are far too complex to be explained in full here. Politics had a good deal to do with it, and the position of London's public transport system, operating not only under the critical eye of the citizens and local politicians of the

metropolis but also having to contend with the national press and Parliament, is much more exposed to what could be heavy pressure than operators elsewhere in the country.

On a more practical level, London's position as a national and international tourist centre also influenced its experience of conductor-less buses. Hitherto, the conductor had been guide as well as fare collector and this sometimes had a major effect on operating schedules, as passengers requested information from drivers and thereby halted the loading process. Yet even on routes where most passengers were regulars, loading on the Daimler Fleetline buses with their turnstile self-service system intended for such people while others were left to deal with the driver, was very slow. It was by no means uncommon in the morning rush hour for a Fleetline to be held up at a stop outside a main-line railway terminal for up to 4min as the queue of intending passengers was cleared barely any faster than it was being added to by

Left:
The Routemaster has produced a remarkable degree of commitment by other operators to the London Transport RM series of fleet numbers, even to the extent of inventing them. When dealer Brakell of Cheam acquired some of the ex-Northern vehicles in December 1977, it was decided to repaint two of them which were in good order into full London Transport livery for use on the Round London Sightseeing Tour, on which LTE often used hired vehicles. They were given fleet numbers RMF2761 and 2762, to follow on from the last example of the model delivered new to LT, RML2760, and EUP 407B is seen in May 1979 while running as RMF2762 at the Victoria terminus of the tour. Later that year London Transport itself began buying ex-NGT Routemasters and, not having any record of the Brakell use of the numbers, also issued RMF2761 upwards. To avoid confusion, the independently-owned vehicles became RMF2791 upwards. *M. G. Fitzgerald*

further people coming from the trains. Even if the inspector intervened to get the bus away before it was completely full, a couple of Routemasters on another route covering some of the same destinations would probably have gone by, and one did not have to be a bus enthusiast to decide that services run by the older model were a better bet if getting to work on time was the aim.

In fact, the idea of converting further central bus routes to one-man working was abandoned, and the 1974 Fleetline order was altered to include 460 of this model which were to be run with conductors. Even so, this decision, coupled with the continuing good reliability of the Routemaster, meant that the model was set for a further spell of service. It is amusing to look back to those days and recall the sense of disbelief when it was said that it looked as if Routemaster operation might extend into the 1980s. Admittedly, there were still nearly 1,000 RT-type buses in service in 1974, but the numbers were falling rapidly and they were only surviving because of the shortage of serviceable new buses, aggravated for a time by the effects of the transfer of Fleetline production from the Daimler works at Coventry to Leyland and its combination of delay and gearbox defects built-in when Daimler's techniques were incompletely understood by the new makers. There was also a general slowdown of manufacturing industry around that time caused by the sequence of events in 1973-74 — the Arab-Israeli conflict, the rise in the price of oil, the coal strike and the period of three–day–week working. The last-mentioned had quite a prolonged after-effect as shortages of individual items upset both chassis and body production at a time of high demand, for operators were placing orders for large fleets of new double-deckers to hasten the conversion of driver-only operation, encouraged by the 50% new bus grant.

The change in climate underlined the way in which the Routemaster was being viewed had subtly altered. It was reliable and efficient, save in the need for a person on the rear platform as well as in the driving seat. Although crew operation was still regarded as something to be avoided where possible, and rapidly disappearing in most parts of the country outside London, its continued acceptance as the only practical course for special circumstances of the central London routes removed the Routemaster's major apparent economic weakness.

The model also fitted neatly into London Transport's

Thinking about insurance? GREAT

Facing page:
Although of integral construction, the Routemaster fitted into London Transport's standard overhaul system. Here an RM body shell is dismounted at Aldenham Works in the mid-1960s. The body number B525 chalked on the bulkhead window implies that this was RM525, in the works for its first major overhaul – minor body blemishes have been chalk-marked for attention. The sub-frames were temporarily linked to allow them to be wheeled away for repair or unit exchange on the 'chassis' production line. *LTE*

Left:
Another RM body is seen being moved along the cathedral-like body shop at Aldenham, the great height allowing movement of bodies between the stations appropriate to different stages of repair to be over those already in place. Panels with minor damage have been repaired or replaced, being identifiable by the pink primer paint. This scene was at an open day in 1979. *L. J. Long*

methods of overhauling buses. On the face of things, these were somewhat anachronistic, with the continued principle of removing 'chassis' and 'bodywork' parts of the vehicle from each other and dealing with them separately. There was more logic in this than was at first apparent, in that body repair work, if carried out to the high standard essential if vehicles were to be kept in good order for even a 15-year life, took longer than the rebuilding of a chassis, especially since the major mechanical units were changed on an exchange principle – engines being replaced quite independently of the main vehicle overhauls as condition dictated. Accordingly, LT

had long followed a principle of having a body 'float' – at one time on a basis of 3%, so that there were 103 bodies for every 100 chassis, and chassis were rarely refitted with the same bodywork at overhaul.

Aldenham overhaul works had been opened in 1956 to take over this function from Chiswick, although it was originally intended to serve as a railway works to be connected to the Underground system by a line that was never built. Its equipment and use as a bus overhaul facility was thus being planned at the time when the Routemaster was also at the design and prototype stage, as well as being carried out on the basis of a bus fleet that might amount to 12,000 vehicles. It was thus all on a grand scale, and although the existing bus fleet at that time was based on models with separate chassis, the switch to the Routemaster was very much in mind. In fact, the form of construction of the then new model had been planned with overhaul procedure very much in mind, one of the benefits of operator involvement in design. The system of grouping most of the major units in the assembly of the front sub-frame, effectively half a chassis, went some way towards an ability to follow much the same procedure with the Routemaster as with, say, the RT. The rear suspension assembly, very chassis-like in construction even though pivoted to the body shell, was easly fastened to the front sub-frame by special temporary brackets, and the whole mechanical part of the vehicle, except for the gearbox (which remained attached to the underside of the body shell) could thus be wheeled away for attention in exactly the same way as if it were a true chassis.

The body shell could be not only moved to a part of the works designed to cope with the need for attention to any part of the exterior, but also put on a special jig which enabled it to be tilted if attention was needed to the underside. In fact, as NGT had found under much more severe climatic and heavily salt-laden conditions, corrosion was not a major problem, but the almost inevitable minor accident repairs needed by a fleet operating in city conditions could be dealt with economically – stock of suitable sub-assemblies were held against the probable requirements, either for immediate use in service conditions or to be incorporated as minor dents were picked up at overhaul.

Up to a point, this sequence of overhauls could almost be kept up indefinitely, and with the early production vehicles, their lives have now reached twice those orginally planned. However, some items which passed through early mainten-ance programmes without requiring attention began to need replacement, and throughout, a supply of spare parts to replace expendable items and those beyond economic repair was needed. London Transport, both as a major operator and because of the number of Routemaster buses involved, had considerable 'muscle' in being able to persuade not only AEC but also the makers of individual items to maintain availability of the parts required. Even so, as other models which used the same items gradually became more rare, difficulties began to

be experienced, though sometimes items could be made to specific order, and vehicles withdrawn after major accident damage provided valuable items in some cases.

Meanwhile, the 'outside' users of the Routemaster had all got to the stage of releasing vehicles and hence providing LT with both running vehicles capable of being put into further service and others as sources of spares. The largest was London Country Bus Services Ltd, which had been formed as a subsidiary of the National Bus Company to take over the country (green) and Green Line operations of London Transport where the latter came under the control of the Greater London Council on 1 January 1970. Its basic problem was that of high operating costs inherited in part from its status as part of LT, with higher wage rates than other National Bus Company firms and yet neither the level of traffic nor the source of subsidy to be found in central London and hence available to the London Transport Executive as reconstituted from the same date.

London Country favoured extensive adoption of one-man operation and hence replacement of rear-entrance double-deckers, but there was inheritance of some 487 RT-type models which were the first priority in this regard. In fact, as was the case with LTE itself, the Routemaster was the main 'modern' double-deck strength, as there were at that date only eight Daimler Fleetline and three Leyland Atlantean models capable of one-man operation. The LCBS Routemaster fleet consisted of 97 RML buses (the original allocation of 100 having been cut by three that were transferred to the central area in 1969, in exchange for the three Atlanteans) the 68 RMC Routemaster coaches plus the former CRL4, by then also classified RMC, and the 43 RCL coaches. They continued in LCBS with little drama through the early and mid-1970s beyond changes of livery, the initial sign of the breakaway from LT being a switch to a brighter yellow for the relief colour band on the RML buses – there was also a new logo which always reminded the author of a telephone, also added to the coaches which initially did not change in colour. However, in 1972 new AEC Reliance single-deckers without conductors replaced the Routemaster coaches on all but one peak-hour service (the 709 from Godstone to London, for which three vehicles were retained until 1976 when they too gave way to single-deckers, in this case Leyland Nationals). The displaced coaches were repainted in bus livery, initially the traditional London Country area green with the yellow band.

Towards the end of 1972, the National Bus Company introduced its corporate livery, individual operating companies being required to adopt either a standard red or green with white relief. LCBS naturally remained a user of green, but the shade became the markedly brighter National Bus Company leaf green and in the case of the Routemasters the relief colour continued to be the standard between-decks band, now in white. Wheels, in standard NBC fashion, were grey.

LCBS pressed on with its programme of conversion of services to driver-only operation, and in the mid-1970s sizeable fleets of new Leyland Atlantean and Leyland National buses enabled quite a number of Routemasters to be taken out of service. The disruption of the three-day week in industry and the consequent spares shortage had led to some being used as sources of parts to keep other buses in service, and some vehicles had become derelict to varying degrees. In December 1977, agreement was reached between LCBS and LTE for the latter to purchase almost the whole fleet of the former's Routemasters, and transfers began almost immediately, continuing until 1980. All but two of the RML buses were purchased but only 78 were repainted red for service, with whatever repair work necessary carried out. The remaining 17 were dismantled for spares and the remains sold to Wombwell Diesels, the well-known vehicle breakers based in Yorkshire, which concern had already received the two not included in the LCBS-LTE deal – they were in fact bought from Wombwell by LT, again for spares. The RML buses needed little modification work to make them suitable for central London, though the gearboxes were converted to fully-automatic control.

The shorter RMC coaches, all of which returned to LT ownership, apart from the prototype, RMC4, were mostly put to use as trainers, none re-entering passenger service, and withdrawals of these began in 1981. The longer RCL versions were also mainly intended to be used as trainers and for other non-passenger services, one becoming a mobile cinema. In the event, two were scrapped but the remaining 40 were, after all, put into passenger service, retaining their 65 coach seats but with the platform doors and luggage racks removed – they also lost their twin-headlamp front wings in favour of standard Routemaster items, but the air suspension and high-geared rear axles were not converted unless new units were needed for repair reasons.

The vehicles put back into passenger service retained their original fleet numbers, and the RCL versions retained that prefix even though used on normal red bus duties.

However, these were not the first coach-like Routemasters to find their way on to normal London bus duties. When the need for the British Airways fleet diminished and then vanished with the phasing out of the Gloucester Road premises as a customs and check-in point, it was agreed that London Transport would purchase the vehicles which became surplus. The first stage resulted from a BA reorganisation before the terminal closed, and 13 of the Routemasters were sold to LT in 1975. They were converted for passenger service on a normal route (175 from Romford garage) by adding bell cords and removing the luggage racks, though somewhat unusually for LT the destination display arrangements were decidedly rudimentary, with no more than destination boards in the nearside bulkhead window and slightly later, a route number box under the canopy. A new fleet number series was used with the prefix RMA, the initial purchase becoming RMA1-13.

Some entered service on the route in October 1975, at first in BA red livery, although a start was made on repainting them in standard LT red style. However, complaints from crews, mainly on the lack of grab handles, led to their withdrawal from passenger service after less than a year in September 1976, the route reverting to RT-type buses. The logic of this capitulation seems a little difficult to follow in the more robust climate of 1989, particularly as Northern General had been operating its forward-entrance Routemasters without any reported difficulty for a dozen years at that date, but LT was still following what amounted to a policy of giving in to staff demands of that type on the basis that industrial problems would prove more catastrophic. So it was agreed that the RMA class would be used as trainers or for staff transport and despite the non-public use, the entire batch of ex-British Airways vehicles were given numbers in this series, RMA14-27 being issued in 1977 and RMA28-65 in 1979. Each renumbering was in order of the original registration numbers of the vehicles concerned, but the fact that these were selected on other grounds meant that the overall original order became disrupted.

Apart from the migrations of vehicles from and to LT stock, the overall service life of the Routemasters has been remarkably uneventful in view of the long periods of use achieved. It is something of an indication of the sound construction and well-planned maintenance system that it simply went on . . . and on . . . and on. The main items to catch the enthusiasts' and the public's eye over the years have been the various non-standard liveries as well as, to a lesser degree, the relatively minor changes in the standard London colour schemes and lettering.

Overall advertising was an idea which was pioneered by London Transport in 1969. Its eye-catching effect was such that all-over advertisement buses appeared to be quite numerous in the period between then and 1976, when the general scheme was dropped. In fact, only 30 Routemasters appeared in this style between these years and as none of them ran for more than two years and some for as few as four months, the numbers were even smaller at any given time. Among them were three RMC vehicles, by then owned by London Country. The idea was always controversial, and particularly so in London, where the concept that buses should be red was part of tourist folklore alongside the images of the London policeman and the Yeomen of the Guard. There was also the fact that the effectiveness of the all-over advertising would have been diminished if such vehicles had ever been allowed to become commonplace – and indeed, the element of novelty of such vehicles in general had diminished noticeably by the mid-1970s.

Although it was announced that no more such advertisements were to be carried by London Transport buses, exceptions did follow, doubtless as the pressure on finances became more acute, and the temptation of earning any form of revenue stronger. One appeared in 1980 and at the end of 1983, overall advert Routemasters began to reappear.

However, a more co-ordinated type of venture had materialised meanwhile. The Silver Jubilee year, 1977, provided an opportunity to combine a fitting contribution to the general air of celebration on London's streets with an opportunity for commercial sponsorship. Appropriately, 25 RM-type buses appeared in an almost all-silver livery to mark the 25th year of the Queen's reign, each carrying advertising of the sponsor. They were temporarily renumbered SRM1-25, all being drawn from vehicles built in 1963-64 which were going through overhaul at the time, reverting to their normal numbers between RM1648 and RM1922 when they were repainted red after the April-November period of use. At first glance, they were reminiscent of an earlier bus, RM664, which had been delivered with its aluminium panels unpainted in an experiment to see whether this might be acceptable for general use. It was not, unlike the parallel switch to unpainted tube train rolling stock, and thus RM664 had been painted red in 1965 – the Silver Jubilee buses were *painted* silver, needless to say. Two more buses, RM2 and RM442, had also been painted similarly in experimental tests before the SRM exercise, but had not run in service or been renumbered.

RM2 was used again for an experimental livery trial, during 1977, this time for the 150th anniversary of Shillibeer's horsebus service of 1829 generally accepted as the prototype of multi-stop bus services in Britain. This time 12 buses were involved, again with advertising sponsorship, and they appeared in a green, yellow and red livery bearing the word 'Omnibus' which was a rather free adaptation of the original. Also in 1979, a further 16 RM buses were painted in a special red and yellow livery to operate a West End circular service known as the Shoplinker. Apart from the lowest-numbered Shoplinker, RM59, the buses in both these exercises were numbered between RM2130 and 2207, again reflecting those going through overhaul at the time. The Shoplinker proved unsuccessful and thus lasted no longer than the anniversary liveries.

The next special livery to appear celebrated the wedding of the Prince of Wales, the vehicles being red with a giant silver 'ribbon' complete with bow. In this case, eight vehicles appeared in service, plus, once more, a prototype used to develop the idea and to show to potential sponsors. This time the overhaul programme caused quite early vehicles to be involved with numbers between RM219 and RM607.

In 1983, the golden jubilee of London Transport itself came round, and four Routemasters were painted in as close an approximation to the 1933 livery as the styling of the Routemaster allowed, with red and white as the main colours, with silver roof and black relief. It looked remarkably attractive, though it is fair to say that the RM body design seems to be one that lends itself to a wide variety of styles. In addition to RM8, RM17, RM1933 (appropriately) and RM2116, another apt bus, RM1983, was painted gold.

CHAPTER SIX

ROUTEMASTER RENAISSANCE

It seems more than a little ironical that it was a political upheaval that caused the routine withdrawal of Routemasters to begin, even though the type had already built up an outstanding record for longevity of service. The pros and cons of alternative policies on fares and subsidies form too large a subject to justify a detailed exposition in this volume. Briefly, however, London Transport's fares were increased twice in 1980 to catch up with costs, and for an election of the Greater London Council in May 1981, the Labour Party included proposals for this policy to be reversed. In its manifesto, the 'Fares Fair' programme was put forward, with plans for a 25% cut in fares and other concessions.

Labour won that GLC election and after taking office called upon London Transport to implement the change of policy in accordance with the system that had been in force since 1970 under which the LTE was under GLC control on matters of major policy. In fact, the Fares Fair ideas were carried even further than had been promised, with fare cuts averaging 32% introduced in October 1981. The number of passengers carried on LTE buses and trains daily increased from 5½ to 6 million, with slight but useful reduction in the use of cars and hence traffic congestion.

Inevitably, however, there was a cost and the subsidy to London Transport rose to £125 million per annum. Ratepayers protested even though quite a large proportion of the subsidy was met by central Government. Bromley Borough Council contested the legality of the new policy in the courts and the outcome was that it was declared to be unlawful. Reluctantly, new proposals to meet the ruling were drawn up and fares were almost doubled in March 1982, making them about a third higher than they had been just before Fares Fair had been introduced. Passengers carried dropped again to 5 million per day, and inevitably cuts in the fleet were the result.

It was decided to withdraw 200 Routemasters, a step that would probably not have been taken until five years later had Fares Fair survived. Thus 'normal' London Transport withdrawal of Routemasters began towards the end of 1982; the earlier special cases such as fire or accident victims or the vehicles acquired as non-runners from London Country had been scrapped by force of circumstance. On the face of things, this was very understandable and certainly no disgrace when it is borne in mind that the early examples were already about 23 years old. Moreover, most other major operators had been withdrawing front-engined double-deckers of similar age from about the mid-1970s simply because they were uneconomic due to the need for crew operation. Circumstances in London had been different, but the climate of new emphasis on operating economy made it seem likely that the capital would have to fall in line with accepted practice elsewhere.

Indeed, it was heavy cuts in services dictated by economics that made withdrawal of Routemasters seem a logical step. As it was, they had survived many later and superficially more up-to-date types, including the rear-engined AEC Merlin and Swift single-deckers and many of the Daimler Fleetline double-deckers. The latter had been snapped up by many operators and such was the availability of relatively modern rear-engined double-deckers at attractively low prices that the prospects for sale of Routemasters for further use as buses to carry fare-paying or even non-paying passengers seemed remote, at any rate in Britain. Most of the early surplus vehicles

numbers of vehicles sold were not, as might have been expected, concentrated towards the low figures but even in the early batches, spread over much of the main RM series.

Up to 1985, the withdrawn vehicles' fate was largely as expected — generally scrap, apart from limited numbers sold for export, non-PSV use or in a few cases, preservation. It was hoped that China might be a promising market, and RM1288 was rebuilt with 'left-handed' rear-end, moving the entrance platform to the right-hand side, with a view to encouraging such a deal in 1984. However, the major sea-change on the basic principles of bus route licensing made by the Transport Act of 1985 was to open up unexpected opportunities.

Significantly, it was a then relatively unknown independent operator based in Perth, Stagecoach Ltd, which purchased five Routemasters in January 1985, soon followed by five more, before the drastically altered legislation had gone through Parliament. Hitherto, Scotland was without any buses of this type but it was set to become the scene of the model's renaissance although it was not to be long before Routemasters became liable to appear in any part of Great Britain where they were seen as an effective way of competing in the new battle for passengers. For it was the very fact that they were designed for crew operation, so long the perceived drawback of the model, that made them attractive. Fast loading and the elimination of the need for passengers to have correct change or suffer the wrath of an unsympathetic driver's tongue could now be used as a means of taking passengers unwilling to put up with these irritations of the pay-as-you-enter system.

In fairness, English independent operators had begun to see what the Routemaster could offer, but Stevenson's of Uttoxeter's pioneer venture in this regard was based on an ex-NGT forward-entrance example and the special case of Obsolete Fleet, the London-based concern running old London buses on a commercial but enthusiast-orientated basis was hardly representative. Later in 1985, Clydeside Scottish Omnibuses Ltd, one of the newly-formed subsidiaries of the Scottish Bus Group in its restructuring carried out in June of that year (aimed at making the group more able to work effectively in the forthcoming competitive environment) began adding Route-masters to its fleet. Like those of Stagecoach, these were standard ex-LT RM-type buses and the initial interest did not indicate the importance of what was to follow. One vehicle, RM652, had been borrowed in connection with an open day, along

went to scrap dealers, though a couple were sent on a sales trip to the United States and Canada, bringing in a few sales among operators who had used earlier London buses.

Early vehicles selected for sale were generally those which had Leyland engines, but by 1985 the criterion was altered to put the emphasis on those due for their fifth body overhaul — incidentally the principle of lifting the body shell from the chassis items was given up from June 1984, the last vehicle to be so treated being RM198. Incidentally, the individual vehicle with two other old-style vehicles, but was retained for a further week, during which it operated on all-day services from most of Clydeside's garages, notably on commuter routes into Glasgow.

There had been a long history of intense rivalry between the Scottish Bus Group (SBG) and Strathclyde Passenger Transport Executive and their respective predecessors and the prospect of direct competition led operators in the area around Glasgow to review their operating policies. As well as Clydeside, the SBG had created another new offshoot, also operating into the area, Kelvin Scottish, and somewhat similarly, Strathtay Scottish had been formed with an area which took it into the district around Dundee, where the local ex-municipal services were run by Tayside Regional Council, again with the likelihood of competition. The trials with RM652 continued when Kelvin borrowed it, and the immediate outcome was that Clydeside placed an order for 12 RMs, of which RM652 and another bus borrowed to extend the experiment, RM694, were part. Then it was announced that Kelvin was to have 59 and Strathtay ordered 20, but these were part of a larger SBG order for 137 which included a further 46 for Clydeside as well as its initial dozen.

What was in mind was the need to build up suitable fleets for the onset of competition, and delivery continued steadily through the early months of 1986. Deregulation day was to be 26 October, but in effect in the Glasgow area the beginning of competition was 31 August 1986, for Kelvin and Clydeside introduced the services planned for the new circumstances under the existing licensing system on that date. Many of the Routemasters were in service, and the concentration of interest in the Glasgow area also led Stagecoach to set up a new company, Magicbus (Scotland) Ltd, to which most of its Routemasters, hitherto used on local contract, school and rural services around Perth, went to the Glasgow area for operation on new Magicbus routes from 26 October. However, delivery of the SBG order was still far from complete at that stage and continued until February 1987.

To varying extent, operators tended to regard the Routemasters as a special purchase for the exceptional circumstances of the time. As old — indeed very old — vehicles by normal standards, it was not expected that they would remain in service for long, yet it was found that basic reliability was comparable with much more modern types, give or take minor problems and the question of continued spares

availability. Fuel consumption is generally much better than that of modern rear-engined models, largely thanks to the low weight, but crew costs have to be set against that, and indeed the low seating capacity by modern standards of 64 is another factor. Yet the fast loading, and the popularity of conductored buses with the travelling public, helps to keep those seats occupied by fare-paying passengers at a faster rate than slow-loading driver-operated big-capacity buses and this can be a major factor in the right circumstances.

Interest in the RM as a possible weapon in the competitive bus 'wars' took a little longer to develop in England and the Scottish upsurge of interest tended to be considered as an exception to the general pattern in the 1985-86 period, for the most part. The possibility of the China deal coming off was still in mind, with talk of as many as 1,300 as a feasible total, and Sri Lanka, once a customer for sold-off RTs and earlier buses, was also seen as a possible big user. The number of RM-type buses in stock with London Buses Ltd (the owners of the ex-LTE fleet from April 1985, following the brief period of direct ownership by London Regional Transport) had fallen to 1,357 by the end of 1985, though the RML fleet was still virtually complete at roundly 500.

For a while, there was a continuing tendency to regard the Routemaster as obsolete in the sense that London route conversions to driver-only operation were being carried out as fast as possible to reduce operating costs. However, the major routes running into and across central London remained very largely operated by Routemasters. Growing awareness of the need for public acceptance of London bus policy if the principle of enterprise and, ultimately, deregulation was to be applied, made something of a conflict of trends.

Meanwhile, there were developments relating to the London fleet, bringing a degree of variety if at the expense of the traditional sense of tidiness so long associated with London buses. A scheme using a yellow roof to publicise particular routes led to another in 1986 in which a yellow band just above upper-deck cantrail level was introduced to help in identifying routes thought to be of special interest to visitors to the capital. The commercial value of the registration numbers carried by Routemasters placed in service up to 1963 was realised and several were either sold off or transferred to later vehicles. Curiously they received A-suffix marks, RM56 becoming XMC 223A instead of VLT 56, for example. In a sense, this was incorrect, as it implied that the bus dated from 1963 rather than

Facing page:
When withdrawal of Routemasters began on a regular basis towards the end of 1982 it did not seem likely that many would see further service in Britain. China was seen as a promising market for the type and a prototype conversion was carried out on RM1288, with staircase and entrance reversed in a similar manner to an exercise that had been carried out on RT-type vehicles with export sales in mind, but in this case with full-depth sliding windows as an additional feature. The vehicle is seen as rebuilt in October 1984. *R. Bailey*

1959. It also introduced the rare A-suffix, only used to a limited extent as the system was just being started, hitherto not to be found on a London bus. Kelvin Scottish also transferred several ex-Routemaster registrations to modern coaches as a ploy to hide their true age in the manner now common.

Sales to English operators began to gain momentum early in 1986 when Blackpool Borough Council bought an initial batch of four RMs after trials with one vehicle. In that case, the purchase was influenced by experience with rear-entrance Leyland Titan PD3 buses, some of which had been retained and which had proved more reliable than later types as well as quite popular with the public.

In London, the public interest value of the Routemaster was acknowledged at about the same time by the announcement that 50 were to be used on sightseeing work from the summer of 1986. The initial selection comprised 39 RMs and the 11 remaining RCL coach Routemasters still in the fleet. All were being repainted in traditional London Transport livery, a somewhat ironical decision as only a few months earlier it had been laid down that the 'showbus' vehicles taken to rallies by several London garages could no longer be in obsolete variations of livery on the rather thin argument that when in public service they caused confusion to the public. The sightseeing fleet was to include 20 open-top vehicles. Subsequently, another variety of coach-seated Routemaster was recruited to join the sightseeing fleet when some of the RMA class of ex-British Airways vehicles were transferred. The fact that they had platform doors was found to be helpful in avoiding intending passengers for normal services boarding the sightseeing vehicles by mistake, a common problem with the standard vehicles when on this duty.

As deregulation of bus services outside London began to take effect, local competitive ventures and rivalry occurred in various places. One was Southampton, where the municipally-owned company which ran the former council buses, Southampton City Transport Co Ltd, decided to purchase Routemasters after trials with one, adopting a red livery but with the relief band in cream and deepened to just above lower-deck window level for the 12 buses placed in service in the summer of 1987. Verwood Transport, based at a village near Bournemouth but operating into Southampton, purchased RMA11, fitting it with a destination box for the first time and modifying the cab slightly to allow it to be used on a driver-only basis. A further stage in Stagecoach's progress was the purchase of Cumberland Motor Services in July 1987, and RMs soon duly appeared on the streets of Carlisle.

Several of the operators which had purchased Routemasters added more to their fleets, often in addition to vehicles acquired as a source of spares. There was also a steady trickle of sales to dealers of vehicles mainly intended for scrap as well as occasional sales overseas or for non-passenger use. Those remaining in London services were often looking rather shabby by the summer of 1987, but then towards the end of the year it became official policy that the RMLs at least would survive on central routes into the era of deregulation, although that tended to drift a little further into the future than had been thought. Among the surviving vehicles of the more unusual varieties, two of the RMC coaches came into the news — none had been used in normal public service since London Country withdrew its last examples in 1980, but RMC1491 was repainted for use by London Coaches Ltd, the name given to the 'leisure' side of the ex-LT business. RMC1515 was converted to an open-topper and operated in this form on Route 15.

By early 1988, the number of standard RMs on regular Monday to Friday workings was down to less than 300, a total of some 450 vehicles having been withdrawn during the previous year. On the other hand, the RML stock position still stood at 503.

With the intention of keeping the model in service for some time to come, the idea of re-engining was re-examined. Towards the end of the GLC era, there had been a plan to fit Gardner engines, abandoned when the change of policy and reorganisation brought the decision to make big cuts in the fleet. Now the question was reopened, and experimental installations of DAF and Iveco engines made. RM545 received a DAF engine and RM1854 an Iveco unit, both entering regular service in this form on Route 2B in the autumn of 1988. Although a typical bus engine can be overhauled and brought back to virtually as-new standards by replacing wearing parts many times, some erosion of items like cylinder blocks by the circulation of cooling water does occur and some of the AEC AV590 engines in the Routemasters are getting to the stage where very little of the original unit remains and further replacements are becoming difficult to obtain or would imply a disproportionate expense in new tooling, which is uneconomic on a unit long obsolete for other purposes.

Meanwhile, further new customers were being found for sold

examples. In November 1987, the United Counties Omnibus Co - Ltd (UCOC) was another concern to be taken over by Stagecoach, and, sure enough, only a few months went by before eight RMs were ordered for UCOC use in the Corby area, later followed by others as well as repeat batches for various other fleets from Strathtay to Southampton. Then in the spring of 1988, East Yorkshire Motor Services Ltd (EYMS), another ex-National Bus Company concern, in this case now run by a management buy-out team, ordered eight RMs for operation in the Hull area. These were of interest in the revival of EYMS' traditional livery of dark blue with three cream bands, a very traditional style which proved to look unexpectedly attractive on the RM. A local independent concern, Citibus, also took an RM for operation in Hull.

Later in the year it was announced that Sri Lanka was to take 40 RMs, far fewer than had been forecast at one stage but still a substantial number from the dwindling stocks of vehicles on offer. Southend Transport took 12 but possibly the most interesting was Greater Manchester Buses Ltd's order for 10, painted in red and white and thus looking very much as in London service yet also subtly reminiscent of the Manchester Corporation red of pre-PTE days. The fact that there is a Piccadilly in Manchester as well as London was exploited to add to the London look by describing the route as the Piccadilly Line linking the town terminal so named with West Didsbury. Another ex-municipal user in the North West was Burnley & Pendle, which took delivery of RM2133 and others towards the end of the year. Another export batch was earmarked for Japan, taking 30 vehicles.

Back in London, it was made clear early in 1988 that no further conversions to driver-only operation beyond those already announced were to occur, with Routemaster operation set to continue indefinitely. A major repainting campaign was intended to improve the look of the fleet, and although other types received a modified livery including a grey strip along the lower edge of the side panels, the Routemaster version is toned down to make only the lifeguard rail grey and thus the traditional look is retained virtually unaltered, apart from the new London Buses bull's eye motif. At a press conference toward the end of the year, Norman Cohen, LBL's director of operations, was able to report that the fleet of RM and RML buses still in service was in remarkably good shape and had just benefited from the refurbishing programme.

So it seems clear that the Routemaster will remain a familiar sight in central London for some time yet, quite apart from the examples of the model still to be seen elsewhere. Some may cease, as did Southampton's operation of the type in January 1989, but others are set to continue for some little time at least. In this regard, it is perhaps significant that Clydeside Scottish purchased RML900, which was in a damaged state and not expected to see service again, repaired it to a high standard and felt sufficiently proud of the result to christen it *Clydesider*, sending it back to London on a courtesy rally visit.

A clear indication of the Routemaster's continuing potential for the future was the formation in 1989 of the Routemaster Operator's and Owner's Association, with 17 operator members and 28 owners of preserved vehicles — it was reckoned that about 1,350 Routemasters were still in operational service. London Buses has continued its search for alternative engines with Cummins C-type and Volvo installations. In November 1989 it was announced that engines of Leyland designs built in India and Poland, were also being considered — it was claimed that the Polish version, made by Pezetel, was virtually identical to a British-built 680, which was the larger capacity version of the Leyland 600 fitted to some Routemasters from new.

In the event, orders were announced in March 1990 for 264 Cummins C-series 8.3-litre engines and 150 Iveco 836/1 8.2-litre engines to replace the existing units in RMLs. Although of smaller capacity than the AEC AV590, and being supplied in considerably derated non-turbocharged form to obviate the need for transmission changes, they will give slightly more power, the Cummins developing 134bhp at 1,800rpm and the Iveco a similar figure. Another intriguing event is the rebuilding of open-top RM163 by LBL's London Coaches subsidiary with a full-length extra bay, making it over 32ft long. The long wheelbase may discourage wider use of the latter idea, but both events convey the continuing high regard for the model.

Early production examples of the model are now 30 years old and yet some at least seem likely to go on for quite a while. Had it been suggested in 1959 that this would occur, even the most optimistic fan would have felt bound to dismiss the idea with incredulity. And going back a little further, I can recall thinking that, when I saw RM1 leave the AEC works at Southall for its first public appearance in 1954, it wouldn't last as long as the dear old RT, bearing in mind its new-fangled lightweight integral construction. How very wrong I was!

APPENDICES

Appendix 1

Prototypes (all built for London Transport)

Fleet No	Registration	Code	Body structure	Running gear	Engine (as built)	Chassis No	Seating	Date built	Date into service
RM1	SLT 56	1RM1	LTE/PR	AEC	AEC 9.6-litre	RM1	H36/28R	1954	February 1956
RM2	SLT 57	2RM2	LTE/PR	AEC	AEC AV470	RM2	H36/28R	1955	May 1957
RML3	SLT 58	3RM3	Weymann	Leyland	Leyland O.600	RML3	H36/28R	1957	June 1957
CRL4	SLT 59	4RM4	ECW	Leyland	Leyland O.600	CRL4	H32/25RD	1957	July 1957
FRM1	KGY 4D	10RM11	Park Royal	AEC	AEC AV691	FRM1	H41/31F	1966	June 1967

Notes:

RM1 originally bore registration OLD 862 but was re-registered as shown before entering service.

RM2 was originally allocated registration OLD 863 but was re-registered as shown before entering service and the AV470 engine was replaced by a 9.6-litre unit. At first painted country area green, it was repainted red for central area service, reappearing in service in September 1957.

RML3 was renumbered RM3 in August 1961 when RML was adopted as the fleet number prefix for the 'lengthened' 30ft version of the Routemaster.

CRL4, built as a prototype Green Line coach version of the type, was renumbered RMC4 in August 1961, this prefix also being adopted for the production Green Line version of 1962.

Appendix 2

Production vehicles (all with Park Royal body structures and AEC running gear but engines as shown)

Operator	Fleet No	Registration	Code	Engine (as built)	Chassis No	Seating	Date built
LT	RM5-300	VLT 5-300	5RM5	AEC AV590	*see notes*	H36/28R	1958-60
LT	RM301-631	WLT 301-631	5RM5	AEC AV590	*see notes*	H36/28R	1960-61
LT	RM632	WLT 632	5RM5	Leyland O.600	2R2RH 628	H36/28R	1961
LT	RM633-869	WLT 633-869	5RM5	AEC AV590	*see notes*	H36/28R	1961
LT	RM870	WLT 870	5RM5	Leyland O.600	2R2RH 866	H36/28R	1961
LT	RM871-879	WLT 871-879	5RM5	AEC AV590	R2RH 867-875	H36/28R	1961
LT	RML880-903	WLT 880-903	7RM7	AEC AV590	R2RH/1/876-899	H40/32R	1961-62
LT	RM904-999	WLT 904-999	5RM5	AEC AV590	R2RH 900-995	H36/28R	1961
LT	RM1000	100 BXL	5RM5	AEC AV590	R2RH 996	H36/28R	1961
LT	RM1001-1008	1-8 CLT	5RM5	AEC AV590	R2RH 997-1004	H36/28R	1961
LT	RM1009	9 CLT	5RM5	Leyland O.600	2R2RH 1005	H36/28R	1961
LT	RM1010-1253	10-253 CLT	5EM5	AEC AV590	R2RH 1006-1249	H36/28R	1961-62
LT	RMF 1254	254 CLT	7RM8	AEC AV590	3R2RH 1250	H31/38F	1962
LT	RM1255-1452	255-452 CLT	5RM5	Leyland O.600	2R2RH 1251-1448	H36/28R	1962-63
LT (GL)	RMC1453-1520	453-530 CLT	6RM6	AEC AV590	R2RH1449-1516	H32/25RD	1962
LT	RM1521-1600	521-600 CLT	5RM5	Leyland O.600	2R2RH1517-1596	H36/28R	1963
LT	RM1601-1719	601-719 DYE	5RM5	Leyland O.600	2R2RH1597-1715	H36/28R	1963
LT	RM1720-1810	720-810 DYE	5RM5 or 9	AEC AV590	R2RH1716-1806	H36/28R	1963-64
LT	RM1811-1865	811-865 DYE	5RM9	Leyland O.600	2R2RH1807-1861	H36/28R	1964
LT	RM1866-1985	ALD 866-985B	5RM9	Leyland O.600	2R2RH1862-1981	H36/28R	1964
LT	RM1986-1999	ALD 986-999B	5RM9	AEC AV590	R2RH1982-1995	H36/28R	1964
LT	RM2000	ALM 200B	5RM9	AEC AV590	R2RH1996	H36/28R	1964
LT	RM2001-2105	ALM 1-105B	5RM9	AEC AV590	R2RH1997-2101	H36/28R	1964
LT	RM2106-2160	CUV 106-160C	5RM9	AEC AV590	R2RH2102-2156	H36/28R	1964-65
NGT	2085-2102	RCN 685-702	—	Leyland O.600	3R2RH2157-2174	H41/31F	1964
LT	RM2161-2217	CUV 161-217C	5RM9	AEC AV590	R2RH2218-2274	H36/28R	1965
LT (GL)	RCL2218-2260	CUV 218-260C	8RM10	AEC AV690	R2RH/1/2175-2217	H36/29RD	1965
LT	RML2261-2305	CUV 261-305C	7RM7	AEC AV590	R2RH/1/2275-2319	H40/32R	1965
LT (CA)	RML2306-2355	CUV 306-355C	7RM7	AEC AV590	R2RH/1/2320-2369	H40/32R	1965
LT	RML2356-2363	CUV 356-363C	7RM7	AEC AV590	R2RH/1/2370-2377	H40/32R	1965
LT	RML2364-2410	JJD 364-410D	7RM7	AEC AV590	R2RH/1/2378-2424	H40/32R	1966
LT (CA)	RML2411-2460	JJD 411-460D	7RM7	AEC AV590	R2RH/1/2425-2474	H40/32R	1966
LT	RML 2461-2598	JJD 461-598D	7RM7	AEC AV590	R2RH/1/2475-2612	H40/32R	1966
NGT	2103	DUP 249B	—	Leyland O.600	3R2RH2613	H41/31F	1964
NGT	2104-2107	EUP 404-407B	—	Leyland O.600	3R2RH2614-2617	H41/31F	1964
NGT	2108-2134	FPT 578-604C	—	Leyland O.600	3R2RH2618-2644	H41/31F	1965
LT	RML2599-2657	NML 599-657E	7RM7	AEC AV590	R2RH/1/2645-2703	H40/32R	1967
LT	RML2658-2760	SMK 658-760F	7MR7	AEC AV590	R2RH/1/2704-2806	H40/32R	1967-68
BEA	1-25	KGJ 601-625D	—	AEC AV690	R2RH/2/2807-2831	H32/24F	1966
BEA	26-65	NMY 626-665E	—	AEC AV690	R2RH/2/2831-2871	H32/24F	1967

Notes:

The codes quoted are the 'basic' ones, following London Transport's standard system of using the figure(s) in front of the type letters to signify 'chassis' variations and those after the letters to signify 'body' variations. Minor differences are indicated by 'stroke' numbers in front of the main chassis code or following the body code. In the case of the Routemaster, this latter practice was used more extensively than usual to indicate variations of electrical equipment, including that for the control of the automatic gearbox, including alternative suppliers of the items involved, some of the items forming part of the 'chassis' assembly and some being included in the body structure. The variations for the standard production RM, basic code 5RM5 ran up to 10/5RM5/10 and, particularly at first, were supplied in quite small batches.

Partly for the reasons quoted in connection with the code system, the batches of chassis numbers allocated to early Routemaster deliveries were out of sequence to some degree, although the first 865 production 'chassis' were used for RM5-869. The first three sets of production chassis units were used under temporary test rig lorry-like vehicles to build up mileage and hence experience in advance of the completed buses, but were then fed back into the production line at Park Royal after that function had been fulfilled, becoming RM459, RM341 and RM398 respectively. Availability of appropriate sets of electrical items 'threw' the sequence at various points between RM253 and RM666.

The relationship between fleet and chassis numbers from RM5 to RM869 was thus as follows:

RM5-252	R2RH004-251
RM253-332	R2RH261-340
RM333-340	R2RH252-259
RM341	R2RH002
RM342-345	R2RH341-344
RM346-397	R2RH361-412
RM398	R2RH003
RM399-446	R2RH413-460
RM447-448	R2RH345-346
RM449-456	R2RH461-468
RM457-458	R2RH347-348
RM459	R2RH001
RM460-463	R2RH349-352

RM464	R3RH260
RM465	R2RH353
RM466-471	R2RH469-474
RM472-478	R2RH354-360
RM479-631	R2RH475-627
RM632	2R2RH628 (Leyland engine)
RM633-658	R2RH629-654
RM659-663	R2RH658-662
RM664-666	R2RH655-657
RM667-869	R2RH663-865

The list of production vehicles is based on the numerical fleet number order of the vehicles built for London Transport, with those built for other operators shown at the appropriate point in terms of chassis number. However, as was often the case with AEC products, the actual order of build was not necessarily the numerical order and the Northern General Transport and British European Airways vehicles were built rather earlier than the numbers suggest. Some of the non-standard London Transport vehicles or batches were also built ahead of numerical order and quite a number of individual vehicles were delayed in entering service, usually because of their being involved in the introduction of new or experimental features.

Appendix 3

Chassis numbers

The sets of mechanical units were given chassis numbers, those for the four prototypes being the same as the complete vehicles as originally built, ie RM1, RM2, RML3 and CRL4. When manufacture of the production versions began at AEC, the sets of units were numbered in accordance with that firm's usual system, beginning at 001 with the AEC-type designation as a prefix. The series continued unbroken by changes of design which caused variation to the prefix, but the tidiness which might have been expected from this and London Transport's usual logical methods was disrupted to some degree by circumstances.

It might have been expected that the first production bus would have been RM5 with chassis number R2RH001 and that subsequent vehicles would similarly be in sequence, the final numbers being out of step by four until the first examples were built for another customer. In a very broad way, this was the general pattern and was actually so between RM479 and RM658, which were R2RH475 to 654, save that RM632, one of the Leyland-engined prototypes, was 2R2RH628 instead of 'plain' R2RH628. The 'four out of step' pattern resumed at RM667 (R2RH663) and continued all the way to RM2160 (R2RH2156), though again there were variations in the prefix because of the changes in 'chassis' design for Leyland-engined RML and RMF variants.

After that, the first order for Northern General Transport broke the pattern for 3R2RH2157-2174 were the first RCN-registered batch, but the resumption of the series for London Transport was with R2RH/1/2175-2217, which were the RCL coaches (RCL2218-2260), and the final standard RM batch RM2161-2217 took chassis numbers R2RH2218-2274. Then came the main production RML batch starting at R2RH/1/2275 with RML2261, but this was broken after RML2598 (R2RH/1/2612) by the second NGT batch which had chassis 3R2RH2613-2644, these being the vehicles with B- and C-suffix registrations. Then RMLs continued to the end with chassis R2RH/1/2645-2806 (RML2599-2760) followed by the British European Airways coach versions which were R2RH/2/2807-2871 in sequence.

The rear-engined Routemaster, FRM1, had a chassis number which was intended to be the beginning of a fresh series, FR2R001.

Appendix 4

Garages

Code	Garage	Vehicles	Total
A	Sutton	DMS (42), RM (33), BL (6)	81
AC	Willesden	RM (32), RML (24), DMS (7)	63
AD	Palmers Green	RM (40), DMS (17)	57
AE	Hendon	DMS (22), RML (21)	43
AF	Putney	RML (39), RM (16), DMS (14)	69
AK	Streatham	RM (58), DMS (9)	67
AL	Merton	DMS (68), RM (57)	125
AM	Plumstead	RM (24), DMS (15)	39
AP	Seven Kings	RM (27), DMS (27)	54
AR	Tottenham	RM (101), DMS (16)	117
AV	Hounslow	LS (51), RM (25), RML (8)	84
AW	Abbey Wood	RM (25), DMS (12)	37
B	Battersea	RM (38), DMS (12)	50
BK	Barking	DMS (54), RM (26), RT (10)	90
BN	Brixton	DM (40), DMS (22), RM (17)	79
BW	Bow	RM (31), RML (31), DMS (18)	80
BX	Bexleyheath	DMS (56)	56
CF	Chalk Farm	DM (37), RM (22), DMS (9)	68
CT	Clapton	RM (36), DMS (18)	54
D	Dalston	RM (47), SMS (11), LS (8)	66
E	Enfield	DMS (55), RM (17), BS (3)	75
ED	Elmers End	LS (28), RM (26), DMS (19)	73
EM	Edmonton	DM (30), DMS (22), RM (15)	67
EW	Edgware	SMS (38), DMS (15), BL (10)	63
FW	Fulwell	DMS (45), RM (18), LS (12), BL (5)	80
FY	Finchley	DMS (25), RML (22), RM (4), FS (2)	53
GM	Victoria	MBA (33), RM (21)	54
H	Hackney	RM (30), RML (26), DMS (10), MBA (8)	74
HD	Harrow Weald	SMS (27), RM (25), LS (7)	59
HL	Hanwell	DM (44), DMS (28), LS (11)	83
HT	Holloway	DM (63), RM (47), RML (28), DMS (26), BS (5), LS (4)	173
HW	Southall	DMS (49), SM/SMS (26), RM (14)	89
K	Kingston	RF (19), BL (16), RM (14)	49
L	Loughton	DMS (26), LS (6)	32
M	Mortlake	RM (34)	34
MH	Muswell Hill	DM (38), DMS (19), LS (10)	67
N	Norwood	RM (58)	58
NB	Norbiton	RM (31), DMS (15), SMS (7), BL (3)	56
NS	North Street	DMS (57), RM (31), BL (5)	93
NX	New Cross	MD (48), RM (45), DMS (34), DM (23), RML (11)	161
ON	Alperton	DMS (39), RM (28)	67
PB	Potters Bar	DMS (18), DM (15), SMS (6), FS (1)	40
PM	Peckham	MD (92), RM (19), DMS (15), LS (13)	139
PR	Poplar	DMS (24), RM (18), LS (12)	54
Q	Camberwell	RM (60), DMS (16), DM (13)	89
R	Riverside	RM (42), BL (4)	46
RD	Hornchurch	DMS (28), LS (18), T (6)	52
S	Shepherds Bush	DMS (32), RM (15), RML (11)	58
SE	Stonebridge	RML (23), DMS (9), RM (8), BA (19)	59
SF	Stamford Hill	RM (22), RML (19), DM (14), DMS (11)	66
SP	Sidcup	DMS (41), RM (36)	77
SW	Stockwell	RM (48), RML (38), DMS (10), DM (8), DMO (6), BS (3), FRM (1)	114
T	Leyton	RM (44), SM (21), RML (20), DMS (20), LS (9)	114
TB	Bromley	RM (34), DMS (30), LS (19), BL (5)	88
TC	Croydon	DMS (57), RM (32), DM (22), BL (5)	116
TH	Thornton Heath	DM (38), DMS (31). SMS (14)	83
TL	Catford	DMS (88), RM (45)	133
U	Upton Park	RML (60), DMS (26), DM (16)	102
UX	Uxbridge	DMS (22), SMS (17), DM (11), BL (2)	52
V	Turnham Green	DMS (18), RM (11), LS (11)	40
W	Cricklewood	DM (37), DMS (30), RM (21), SMS (5), LS (5)	98
WD	Wandsworth	DMS (41), RM (14), DM (9)	64
WH	West Ham	RM (67), DMS (42), DM (13), RML (7), SMS (3)	132
WL	Walworth	RM (29), DMS (21), DM (17), MBA (16)	83
WN	Wood Green	DMS (61), RM (21), DM (10)	92
WW	Walthamstow	DMS (65), RM (18)	83
X	Middle Row	RM (56)	56

The above relates to the position at the beginning of 1979, when the fleet of RM and RML buses delivered for central area services was still virtually intact, apart from four vehicles withdrawn due to accident damage, fire, etc. The former country area Routemaster fleet was in course of transfer from LCBS to LTE, some RMLs having re-entered service, but none of the former coaches, nor the ex-airways Routemasters was then in passenger service with LTE.